Praise for Joe Parkin's previous book,
A Dog in a Hat

"*A Dog in a Hat* is the most authentic book ever written on making a living as a pro cyclist in Europe."
—BOB ROLL, VERSUS TV CYCLING COMMENTATOR

"I loved *A Dog in a Hat*. Joe's stories bring back many memories of racing in Belgium, where I learned how to fight for position in the echelon, to suffer in the gutter while jumping curbs and dodging potholes, and to pound out my guts when it really mattered. Belgium is a hard place to learn bicycle racing, and Joe's story proves how tough he was."
—RON KIEFEL

"This plain, self-deprecating memoir has the ring of authenticity at the other end of the sport where—even today—not all the riders are being paid, the hotels are still bad, and the races are just as hard."
—TINDONKEY.COM

"*A Dog in a Hat* is a page turner. Anyone who has raced in Europe or who wonders what it's like to jump the ocean on your own should pick up this book. Joe captures the struggle and the intensity to succeed, and the fact that he did it on his own is all the more impressive. Cycling in Europe is tough; doing it Joe's way is even tougher!"
—FRANKIE ANDREU

"Joe Parkin is a beautiful piece of work, and he turns out to be a better writer than I am a bike racer."
—BILL STRICKLAND, *BICYCLING* MAGAZINE

"[Readers] have a seat in the middle of the peloton as we see what Joe sees, breathe what he smells, watch as his peers juice up and we struggle with him as he strives to get out in front of it all. Parkin's words weave a colorful tapestry about living life on the bicycle racing circuit in Europe. Yet that tapestry is soiled and tattered because of the true cutthroat nature of bicycle racing and the absolute grit in the stories Joe relives for us."
—*DIRT RAG* MAGAZINE

"Is *A Dog in a Hat* the best book we've ever read about bike racing? Undeniably yes. The essential truths you'll learn about Belgian bike racing are timeless. And the self-effacing (and often hilarious) way Joe narrates the absurdity of these traditions will make you laugh out loud. Of everything written about bike racing throughout the history of mankind, Chapter 3, 'Kermis Don't Play Fair,' is the most important 20 pages ever penned. No one should be permitted to own a USA Cycling license without being able to recite this chapter from heart. You'll be fascinated by Joe's humility, his determination, and by the warped way domestiques set their goals and weigh success."

—COMPETITIVECYCLIST.COM

"*A Dog in a Hat* is funny, touching, brave, and honest in its look at the complicated world of the European pro cycling scene."

—THE *INDEPENDENT* NEWSPAPER

"Parkin has written an eloquent and historic volume. In the very uniqueness of his story, Parkin realizes a universality that gives his recollections a resonance with any cyclist. Do not miss this book."

—BELGIUMKNEEWARMERS.COM

"*A Dog in a Hat* reads like Joe Parkin was just telling you these epic stories on a ride, up a climb, or at a coffee shop. That's the beauty of this book. It's not a hero's journey, but instead a racer's tale."

—BIKEHUGGER.COM

"There's something very approachable about the underdog, the guy who works as hard as anyone, but never achieves the stardom we all chase. I peeled through *A Dog in a Hat* in a few nights, always wanting to know what was coming next. Joe's candor is refreshing to read and entertaining as hell."   —RICHARD PESTES, PEZCYCLINGNEWS.COM

"Written as if you were riding alongside him, Parkin's *A Dog in a Hat* is a quick, highly addictive read. You can feel the cobbles under the pen."

—COG MAGAZINE

"*A Dog in a Hat* reads like a novel and serves up an inspiring, compelling, and captivating racer's tale."   —THE OREGONIAN

"I loved *A Dog in a Hat*. Once in, I couldn't put it down. The book rings of truth, youth, and passion." —ANDREAS HESTLER

"Sordid, funny, and engrossing." —BIKE SNOB NYC

"Joe tells his story straight. It's not pretty, but it's not bitter." —BIKERADAR.COM

"A slice of literary badassness. I've had a lifelong struggle maintaining an attention span for reading books, but this is a page turner that's been hard for me to put down. *A Dog in a Hat* is truly captivating." —HOWTOAVOIDTHEBUMMERLIFE.COM

"Impossible to put down." —*MOUNTAIN BIKE ACTION* MAGAZINE

"Parkin went native in an era when Americans were still exotic creatures, and not in a good way. This unglamorized insider's view is what makes *A Dog in a Hat* well worth reading. Parkin shows you life on the edge of the peloton. We know the great champions' stories, but Parkin's experience is far more illustrative of what a 'pro cyclist' really is." —PODIUMCAFE.COM

"*A Dog in a Hat* is not the idealised notion most of us have of the life of a professional cyclist, but it's all the more gutsy and enjoyable for its self-effacing honesty. I could read it all over again right now." —THEWASHINGMACHINEPOST.NET

"In his new book, *A Dog in a Hat*, Joe Parkin gives us a window into the life of someone who was born to be a professional bike racer. It's not pretty, it's not glamorous, some of it is a bit of inside baseball, but it's a great read. I picked up a copy at Interbike, brought it home and read the 232 pages over the course of two evenings. I literally could not put it down." —SMITHERS MINNEAPOLIS

"The April 17, 2000, issue of *VeloNews* closed with a typically fervent Bob Roll screed entitled '51 Things to Do Before You Die.' '#36. Learn from Joe Parkin's life story.' Parkin's prose fills in all the cracks. Quite simply, the man is tough as nails and chose the absolute hardest way to break into European professional cycling: just showing up in Ghent with a bike, a duffel bag of clothes, three months' worth of cash, and a phone number to call scrawled on a scrap of paper. You can truly appreciate Parkin's re-living of the squalid truth of late '80s Euro pro cycling."

—BOBKESTRUT.COM

"It's a wild, gritty, page-turning ride: Grab the book, rub some embrocation into your quads and calves, and settle into your couch for a great read as you plot your own future bike exploits." —CYCLO-CLUB.COM

"Joe Parkin did what few other Americans dared do. . . . *A Dog in a Hat* fills a void in cycling literature. Since so few Americans have accomplished what Joe Parkin has, his book stands on its own as an original account of European bike racing, presented from a racing cyclist's perspective." —USCYCLINGREPORT.COM

"*A Dog in a Hat* is a fast-paced, revealing read, and any cyclist who enjoys racing will be equally inspired and shocked at some of the stuff that goes on inside the peloton. It's a rare glimpse into a world often concealed, and Parkin's struggle to gain acceptance makes the book a truly inspiring read." —ROADCYCLINGUK.COM

"Written as if you are riding alongside him, this is a quick, highly addictive read. Set in the late eighties, Joe Parkin's tale is of an American who moved to Belgium in order to become a pro racer. Joe's youthful true story documents coming through the ranks of novice riders in pursuit of a professional racing team contract, when Americans in the sport were rare. Quite the no-holds-barred take on professional cycling. Read it if you aren't in denial about what old school pro racing entailed. You can feel the cobbles under the pen. Endorsed by Bob Roll. (What, you need a better endorsement?)" —*COG* MAGAZINE

COME & GONE

COME & GONE

A True Story of Blue-Collar
Bike Racing in America

Joe Parkin

BOULDER, COLORADO

1830 55th Street
Boulder, Colorado 80301-2700 USA
303/440-0601 · Fax 303/444-6788
E-mail velopress@competitorgroup.com

Distributed in the United States and Canada by Ingram Publisher Services

Library of Congress Cataloging-in-Publication Data
Parkin, Joe.
Come and gone: a true story of blue-collar bike racing in America / Joe Parkin.
    p. cm.
    ISBN 978-1-934030-54-7 (pbk.: alk. paper)
1. Parkin, Joe. 2. Cyclists—United States—Biography. 3. Bicycle racing—
United States. 4. Cycling—Anecdotes. I. Title.
GV1051.P37A3 2010
796.62092—dc22
[B]
                        2010006314

For information on purchasing VeloPress books, please call 800/234-8356
or visit www.velopress.com.

Cover and interior design by Anita Koury
Cover illustration © Edel Rodriguez
Photographs are property of the author unless otherwise noted.
Text set in Prensa Book.

10   11   12   /   10   9   8   7   6   5   4   3   2   1

*To Elayna, who reminded me just how
great it is to ride a bike*

CONTENTS

1 Citizen Foreigner   1

2 Philadelphia Flyer   25

3 Silver Bullet   51

4 Texas Broom Wagon   69

5 Paydirt   83

6 Cyclocrossed   97

7 Olympic Dreams   105

8 Chequamegon   131

9 Ooooh, Barracuda   139

10 Come & Gone   163

Epilogue   173

Team History   175

Acknowledgments   177

About the Author   179

1

CITIZEN FOREIGNER

"BESTE JOSÉ," I WROTE AS I HUNCHED OVER IN THE BACKSEAT OF my team's Pontiac Transport minivan. My head was propped against the seat in front of me, and I stared at my lap. "I am writing this letter to thank you for the opportunity to ride for you," I continued in Flemish. We'd just finished a small three-day stage race in North Carolina and were heading out. I knew I would likely never finish the letter, much less mail it, but I was homesick for Belgium and this was the only way I knew how to escape the hell I was experiencing. José de Cauwer had been my boss for the past three years, and although I wouldn't call our relationship anything more than a normal working one, I had an enormous amount of respect for the man who'd barked orders at me from a team car all over Europe.

I stared at the page. Less than a year before, I had been living in Belgium, riding for José's Tulip professional team. Now I was in the southern United States and had just ridden the final criterium of a stage race for little other reason than the fact that we were there. That morning, when we had gone to check the race's general classification, my teammate Tom Armstrong and I had found our names at the bottom of the list. We'd been relegated to last place and next to last and were trying to figure out why. We found a U.S. Cycling Federation (USCF) race official and politely asked if a scoring error might have been responsible for our new spots at the back of the race. After cross-referencing our names and race numbers, the USCF official informed us that we had been disqualified from the previous day's stage because we'd crossed a road's center line.

"Seriously?" I asked, trying my best to stay calm. Ever since I had left for Belgium in the spring of 1986, I'd enjoyed the liberty of using all available road, curbing, sidewalks, and dirt paths while racing. Keeping to the right side of a center line was a whole new obstacle. "I find it interesting that only two of the eight or so pros in this race were busted. The whole peloton was over the line at some point or another yesterday." I knew this was going to be a futile argument.

"You were the ones who were caught," the official explained.

"I find that hard to believe," I countered. He shrugged. Dejected as I was, I would have been content to end the discussion there, but he then told us in which laps our respective crimes had occurred. I had been disqualified at the beginning of the second of eight laps.

"Are you kidding me? Why wasn't I told? I would have quit."

"It would have been unsafe for the motorcycle official to do that," he offered.

It was a lame excuse, in my opinion. I had gotten used to bumping into the hordes of TV, photo, and police motorcycles that work the major races.

"Then you should have yelled at me from the start/finish line."

"You wouldn't have quit," he said.

"Yes, I would have."

"We've tried that before," he explained. "No one ever quits. They just think they can argue their way out of it after the race."

"I would have quit. I think I should have been given the benefit of the doubt." I was fully aware that no reversal of our sentence was going to be granted. The first thing they teach you in umpire school is to never, ever change your call, even if it is the worst one ever made, and I assume USCF officials are given similar advice. He was doing a good job of handling an angry bike racer, and I was doing a pretty good job of being polite, albeit with a dash of condescension.

"I should have been told," I argued again. "It was 100 degrees out there yesterday. I would have quit. I am not out here for my fucking health." I caught a slight hint of confusion in his eyes and began to understand that I was a type of bike racer he had not previously encountered. The notion of intentionally dropping out of a race is foreign to most bicycling enthusiasts. We've all seen the images of Tour de France riders having to endure the ceremonial stripping of the race number from their jerseys before they climb, heartbroken and shamefaced, into the dreaded broom wagon that sweeps the tail of the race. Europe's one-day races, however, are an entirely different scene. If you're not with the leaders, or at least within a giant peloton close to the finish, ending a racer's suffering early is not only commonplace but almost preferred by sponsors and directors. The heroes of the day are out in front showing what they can do, while the workers and also-rans stay out of the public view and rest up for tomorrow.

As I stared at my letter to José, I knew I wouldn't get many more words onto the page. As cruel and inhumane as the racing was in Europe, in many ways it was much harder in the States. In Europe I knew most of the riders I raced against, either from events in which we all competed or from reading about them. In the New World I was learning the names and faces as I went along. From time to time I raced with someone I'd known in Europe or read about in the U.S. magazines, but for the most part I was breaking new ground. In addition, the life of a European bike racer was a fairly simple one: race, eat, get a massage, sleep, eat, and then find your way to a perfectly cleaned bike that your mechanic had carefully parked alongside your teammates' perfectly cleaned bikes. In my freshman year of American pro bike racing, this blessed routine was gone, and I was left to fend for myself. It was terrifying.

My return to the States had come just a few months earlier—October 13, 1991, to be exact. At that point in the year, the season was over for me, and for the first time since turning pro I had no team and no contract for the following year. I wasn't alone. I have always referred to this episode as "the Great Purge of '91" because the pro peloton was reduced by almost 25 percent for the next season. Riders like me, who didn't have a lot of points from the sport's governing body, the Union Cycliste International (UCI), were kicked to the curb because the ones with the points were demanding all the money. And rightly so: If a team could put together a cadre of big-points guys, it could be assured a spot in all of the Grand Tours as well as the Classics. It is a hell of a lot easier to sign huge sponsors when a Tour de France berth is a fact and not just a distant possibility. But just because I understood the business of the thing didn't mean I had to like losing my ride.

When I went to Belgium the first time, I had a big duffel bag full of clothes, my bike, and a spare set of wheels. Now, after hundreds of races against the best cyclists in the world, miles of scar tissue, memories of a hundred crashes, and a working command of several different languages, I was heading to the States with nothing more than a duffel bag and a couple of bikes—bikes that I would come to find were second-rate. When I began my big European adventure, I had a couple of addresses in my pocket but was not completely sure where I would end up living. This trip was not all that different.

That October I headed to Minneapolis, hoping everything would magically fall into place when I got there. I had spent two weeks in Minneapolis the previous July and had gotten to know the guys at the Flanders Brothers bike shop. While I was in Belgium, I'd been keeping in touch with Charlene, my high school girlfriend, who'd visited me in Philadelphia earlier that year. We had laid out a plan for me to stay with her for a while, although it was a vague plan at best. But then she'd gone dark, moving and changing phone numbers after having her apartment burglarized three times in a week, so we had not spoken for several weeks before my flight.

My flight originated in Brussels and landed in Chicago. Having developed the style and mannerisms of a person from northern Europe, I was generally offered the Dutch-language newspapers.

I usually took them, as they would (in most cases) protect me from having to talk with any overenthusiastic American vacationers wanting to educate me in the European history and culture they'd become expert in over the course of the preceding six days. Though I was free from sitting next to any of my fellow Americans, there was a gaggle of them behind me and across the aisle. The most notable of the group was a giant of a man in his 50s or 60s. He spoke slowly and loudly, with a bit of a drawl that suggested he probably came from Oklahoma or Texas. By the way he carried himself, practically swaggering as he sat in his tiny airline seat, I would have bet money that he'd been a good football player back in his day. He was with his wife, I guessed, and several other couples about the same age. I listened as they recounted their trip at a volume so loud that I felt people might also be hearing them from the ground.

This was the first time in years that I had seen a group of traveling Americans, and I was surprised at how much culture shock the experience was giving me. Other than the insane volume level, there was nothing offensive or ugly about these Americans. In fact, I believe I have traveled with more ugly Europeans than ugly Americans. These people were talking about the food and the weather and the buildings they had seen and the beds they had slept in. They missed home and were tired of European food but nevertheless were happy to have experienced other countries and cultures, however touristy their trip had been. As I listened, I began to wonder what it was going to be like to live in a foreign country, even though I had a passport that said I was one of its citizens. I'd spent six years in Ursel, Belgium, more time than in any American town or state I'd ever lived in. My room on the third floor of Albert and Rita Clayes's

Café Sportswereld had become my home, and I wondered how long it would take to become homesick. As I would come to find out, it didn't take long at all.

———

I slotted back into American life slowly, opting to keep my European daily ritual intact. Each day I would get up, have coffee, bread, and jelly, get suited up, and then go for a ride. The problem with cycling in Minnesota in the late fall is that the weather can go from bad to worse in a big hurry. That was exactly what happened at the end of October, when 31 inches of snow dropped on the Twin Cities in just 24 hours. Minnesotans are a tough lot and accepted the snowfall with typical Nordic stoicism. For them, it meant a rare day off from work or school, maybe even a chance to play in the snow. But I was nearly paralyzed. All I could envision was all the hours I would now be spending indoors, riding my bike nowhere atop the training rollers while watching terrible talk shows.

On the day after the big storm, I grabbed my mountain bike and headed off to the Flanders Brothers bike shop to lament the end of riding for the foreseeable future. Much to my surprise, the guys were giddy about this fresh snowfall, explaining that we would now be able to ride on the snowmobile trails. As the son of parents born and raised in Michigan, I had seen snowmobile trails only on trips back to the Motor State, where we had ridden them on one of my cousins' old Ski-Doo or John Deere sleds. I had a hard time picturing bikes on the same trails. The guys straightened me out, though. At the right temperature and with the proper tires, they assured me, a mountain bike could not only ride on top of the snow but could also be a lot of fun. I agreed to trust my new friends and let them prepare my bike for a training ride on snow.

When Sunday arrived, the temperature was pushing into the 20s, with lots of bright sunlight to soften things up further. It seems that the ideal temperature for mountain biking in the snow lies somewhere between 5 and 15 degrees Fahrenheit. Warmer temperatures, though better for my body and overall disposition, are hell for riding. As the temperature inched upward toward freezing, the snow began to melt into a thick, sloppy slurry, making every pedal stroke feel like I was reliving a muddy Paris-Roubaix when my wheel was broken and both brakes were dragging on the rims. The melted snow also created a watery film atop the ice that provided zero traction, and just as on the muddy cobbles of France, suddenly and for no apparent reason the bike would point 90 degrees in a different direction and my body would hit the ground before I had a chance to react. The only part that differentiated the Queen of the Classics from this Sunday ride from Chaska to Belle Plain and back was that the crashes on the snow happened at a top speed somewhere around 18 miles per hour, as opposed to the 20 to 30 that could be expected in the Hell of the North.

I rode this round-trip Chaska—Belle Plain loop almost every weekend from the beginning of October until almost the end of January. The trek always took somewhere in the vicinity of four hours. It did not matter if it was 24 degrees or minus 14 degrees; the ride always lasted about the same amount of time. In warmer temperatures, you had to pick yourself up from a crash every few minutes. In colder temperatures, traction could be incredibly good, but what time we gained in not falling we lost in stopping to get warm. Our hands and toes would lose feeling so fast that we'd stop every few minutes to run and clap our hands together in the hope that some blood and feeling would come back into them. They say every important European race win takes a year off a rider's life. I am pretty sure each snowmobile-trail ride on mountain bikes from Chaska to Belle Plain and back does exactly the same thing.

After the crazy Halloween snowstorm heckled Minnesota in 1991, we road bike riders were treated to some uncharacteristically dry conditions for the remainder of the winter. That meant that we were actually able to ditch the snow riding for road bike riding by the beginning of February. I was a man on a mission to pile up as many miles as possible so I could hit the U.S. racing circuit and make my mark quickly. Almost all the pro bike racers I've ever known possess a creature-of-habit gene that causes them to resist too much exploration, opting instead to train repeat-edly on routes they already know. Being no different, I learned new routes usually only on Sundays, when I rode with the Min-neapolis Bicycle Racing Club (MBRC).

I had grown used to riding alongside any strange combination of pro bike racers in Europe, but riding with the MBRC gang took a little getting used to. In Europe when we were training, riders would pair up and take equal turns riding at the front of the group. In large groups I only had to put my nose out in the wind every hour and a half or so. Our MBRC rides were not the same.

For many, the goal was simply to survive the ride, and they were not following the old Belgian protocol. Others planned to turn off early, cutting the ride to 45 miles. In other words, the military precision of a training ride in Europe was not happening, and my nose was in the wind a lot of the time. At first I was scared that I was going to be working a bunch and then also get worked over at the end, but I didn't, and I grew to like the extra work; it made me feel like I was back in the Tour de Suisse, setting tempo for my team leader as I had done the previous spring.

As the new year of 1992 rolled in, I was beginning to feel a glint of race fitness, but I still didn't have a team. The money I had saved from my Euro team salary and race winnings was running out, and my Tulip team clothing was getting threadbare. In fact, my two-tone green Tulip bib shorts had dime-sized holes where the chamois was stitched to the Lycra, exposing a view of my butt for all of my riding partners to see. I desperately wanted some new clothing and a team, but no one was calling.

Before Johnny Tomac had won the UCI Mountain Bike World Championship in Il Ciocco, Italy, in 1991, he had talked about putting a small team together, including Bob Roll—"Bobke"—and me, to compete in selected road and mountain bike races. Tomac had ridden with the Motorola road team in Europe with Roll, and combining our talents on a stateside team seemed like a good fit. After he won the worlds, though, he became a one-man empire, and any talk of building a team around him disappeared. Bobke became Greg LeMond's Z teammate and sole mountain bike racer. I started thinking about moving over to the mountain bike side of cycling, but never having raced a mountain bike was not helping to open any sponsorship doors. I started thinking about trading in my USPRO professional racing license for an amateur one.

I telephoned the USCF in Colorado Springs to find out if I could regain my amateur status. Without too much button-pushing hassle, I found myself talking with the correct person. I asked if it was possible to obtain a USCF racing license after having had a professional racing license for the previous five years. The nice woman assured me that I would be able to race as an amateur once again, no problem. I jokingly asked if I'd have to start all over as a Category V, the beginner's category.

"No," she explained. "Usually we start you back as a Category II or III. If you feel you should be a Category I, you'll need to submit a résumé for review."

"Serious?" was all I could come up with.

I had never understood the distinction between the top two USCF categories, since they are typically combined at all but about three races on the calendar. I thought it was even stranger that in giving up my professional status to race as an amateur, I'd have to prove my mettle as a bike racer via résumé before being allowed to race in the top amateur category. Imagine a Nextel Cup driver, even one who has never won a Nextel Cup race, being asked to submit a résumé before getting to race in the top category in a Friday-night dirt-track race.

I had stayed in touch with John Eustice over the course of the winter, picking his brain for available rides. John had been one of the American pioneers of European cycling; he had raced in Europe as a 19-year-old junior, turned pro on a French team with Sean Kelly in 1982, and won the first two USPRO Championships in 1982 and '83. I looked to him for advice on returning to the domestic racing scene since he had done it himself. I called John and told him about the conversation that I'd just had with the woman at the USCF.

"Joe, no," he said. "Don't do it. You are a pro. You've been racing as a pro. As long as you want to continue racing, you need
to race with a pro license."

A few days after the conversation with Eustice, I got a call
from Kyle Schmeer, the owner of Cycles BiKyle, a boutique
bicycle shop in Bryn Mawr, Pennsylvania, one of the wealthier
suburbs on Philadelphia's Main Line. With his shop's proceeds
Kyle and a Philadelphia auto dealer, Rip Scott, had been field-
ing a team of professionally licensed cyclists for the CoreStates
USPRO Championship, held on the streets of Philadelphia since
1985. Now they were ready to step up their level of commitment
and have a regionally based pro team campaigning the entire
season. The core squad was to be a small one, made up of Tom
Armstrong, Matt Eaton, Dan Fox, Jeff Rutter, and me. Additional
riders would be brought on board for selected stage races and the
bigger one-day races. The offer from Kyle was a bike, clothing,
shoes, and other equipment and $4,500 for the year.

It was a miserable offer. Had I just returned from Belgium,
that amount of money would have broken me. I know I would
have declined on some misguided principle alone. But now I
just wanted to race again and was being given the opportunity
to do just that. I had already been presented with several better
offers, but all of them were from teams that were still trying to
secure sponsorship, and each offer was contingent on deals being
struck that were out of my control. I slept on Kyle's offer, and I
accepted it the next day.

Riding for Scott/BiKyle required me to go to Philadelphia so
that I could travel with my teammates. I'd hoped that I would
just be able to fly in and out of Minneapolis, meeting up with the
guys in Philly or some other convenient spot, but this was not

going to be part of the deal. There wasn't enough money in the budget for that, so I was expected to base myself in Bryn Mawr for the season. With most of my cash gone, I was forced to buy a one-way Greyhound bus ticket to get me from Minneapolis to Philadelphia. I packed my well-worn Tulip team Koga-Miyata bike in my even older TVM team bike bag, filled my hard-sided suitcase with clothing, stuffed some music, magazines, and other essentials in my backpack, and headed for the bus station. I'd ridden the dog before, mostly on shorter trips such as Minneapolis to Chicago, but this was to be a 34-hour adventure of pain, boredom, and stink, the likes of which I had not previously experienced.

I don't know if it was the time of year or some sick Greyhound promotion, but on every leg of the trip the bus was full. For the most part, Greyhound riders are not adventurous kids with little money or old ladies scared to fly. In fact, most of the people with whom I would share the stale bus air were downright disgusting.

The ride from Minneapolis to Chicago took close to 9 hours and included a snack break at McDonald's in Tomah, Wisconsin. That leg of the trip was the easiest. In Chicago I had to change buses, and the real pain began. Two guys I came to think of as the Smoky Brothers climbed on board in Chicago. I'm pretty sure there's a cigarette-company exec enjoying a yacht moored at some private island somewhere who owes at least a letter of thanks and maybe a free carton of smokes to the brothers for enriching his coffers. At each stop the smoking siblings would suck down as many heaters as possible, practically bathing in the exhaled smoke from their foul-smelling brand of choice. Miraculously, we would somehow find ourselves sitting way too close to each other each time we reboarded the bus after a stop.

For what seemed like the longest stint of the trip, however, I sat next to a very large, very drunk, and very sleepy man who found it completely acceptable to lean his head on my shoulder as he fell asleep and to snore in the direction of my face. In addition to his rank breath, the rest of him exuded a combination of BO, cheap booze, cigarettes, and some other foul funk that I couldn't pinpoint. Each time he nodded off, his mouth would open and his head would tilt in my direction. As soon as I felt hair touch my shoulder, I would elbow the guy in the ribs, he would wake up, and the process would begin again.

I arrived in downtown Philly in the midmorning, tired and a little sore from sitting for so long. The experience reminded me of when I had arrived in Belgium for the first time and had to figure out what to do. As my English was still coming back to me at this point, it even seemed like I was in a foreign country. The overpronounced vowels of Minnesota were now replaced by the choppy accents of the eastern United States. I hopped on a Paoli Local commuter train bound for Bryn Mawr and managed to get off at the right stop. Once on the ground, I walked the quarter mile to Cycles BiKyle, bike bag on my shoulder and suitcase in tow. I am sure Kyle and his employees were not so sure about the pro bike racer they'd hired to represent them when I walked in. I certainly wasn't dressed like a bike racer, and with the weariness in my bones from riding the dog, I looked like a refugee. In many ways, I was.

My teammates and I traveled south to do some racing. It was already past Classics season in Europe—Paris-Roubaix, the Tour of Flanders, and Ghent-Wevelgem were long gone—and I had yet to race my bike. It turned out that the huge amount of miles I'd been riding through the Minneapolis winter wasn't the right way to prepare for American racing. Flogging my legs in the cold and wind might have made me tough, but it was a grinding sort of toughness that would have been good for the Ronde van Vlaanderen or Paris-Roubaix. The southeastern U.S. circuit we'd be tackling was made up of a series of superfast criteriums—circuit races of many laps of a mile or so each, often around downtown squares or office parks. To do well in a U.S. criterium, you had to be pushy and aggressive in the corners and be able to accelerate repeatedly during all the yo-yoing in the pack as it sped up and slowed down for each corner on the course. When I went to Belgium the first time after learning my racing chops on the U.S. crit circuit, I was amazed at how much more slowly the Belgians rode through the corners than the pace I was accustomed to. In fact, I used to shoot up the inside before most turns, taking the front spot just to see what kind of gap I could put on the next guy as I came out of the corner. It was incredible; I could sometimes take as much as four bike lengths without even really pushing it. Back in the States, though, I was now wondering whether my cornering skills had lapsed to beginner levels. In the first race that I rode with my new team, our man Jeff Rutter took the win. Although I was happy for Jeff, I was more than a little concerned that I hadn't lived up to my end of the bargain.

Even though my criterium speed was lacking and my cornering skills a bit rusty, I still kept up my long mileage training program. People—including me—assumed that someone who had raced in the professional ranks in Europe should be able to step back into the domestic racing scene and win races at will. In my case, that simply was not true. I believe that part of my problem was a lack of the familiar flow of the day-to-day life as a bike racer. But I think it was also the fact that despite my birth certificate, passport, and driver's license saying I was an American, I felt like I was in a foreign country. In fact, in America I was like a Belgian who was asked to ride somewhere else. When we traveled from Belgium to any number of lesser races beyond the border, my teammates would lose all motivation to suffer hard enough to perform well. They weren't racing in front of their local fans, and they weren't racing on roads they knew; quite often they simply went through the paces, racing hard enough not to lose face or endanger their jobs but not really caring about the outcome. I had never felt this way when I lived there because, I guess, I considered all of Europe to be my goal. But back home in the States, I was finding that I was not all that motivated.

There was another problem too. In Europe I had a job to do. It was my responsibility to control the race and work for the team. My teams had star riders who relied upon the help I could give them. I didn't have that with the Scott/BiKyle team. It was a great group of guys, and had there been even one star on the team, we would all surely have risen to the occasion.

Meaning and purpose were not far away, however. Our little team was not even on the radar for a spot in the multiday Tour DuPont stage race that had a prize list glitzy enough to attract some of the sport's major teams. But the perfectly respectable Thrift Drug Classic in Pittsburgh, the Kmart Tour of West Virginia, and the CoreStates USPRO Championship in Philadelphia that followed DuPont were on our agenda. Knowing that the guys who had raced the Tour DuPont would all either be flying (in which case they'd be untouchable) or completely wrecked (in which case they'd be dangerous to be around), I wasn't looking at Pittsburgh or West Virginia as anything but training. It was a good thing too because in Pittsburgh I rode about as well as a first-year junior.

West Virginia, on the other hand, was different. After nearly being arrested by a local cop for "playing on *my* highway" while we were out on a training ride, we arrived in Morgantown, West Virginia, and survived the prologue. After a few stages the Coors Light team needed some help. Coors Light had succeeded 7-Eleven as America's top team, and it was stocked with stars— one of whom, Scott Moninger, was now wearing the leader's jersey. Roy Knickman, who was the Coors team's tempo-setting strongman, had been worked over by the Tour DuPont, so Len Pettyjohn, the Coors Light team director, found us. These deals always involve money, but truth be told, I would have ridden myself into a coma just to feel like I had something to contribute to the race. Riding to help protect Moninger's jersey was amazingly motivating—cathartic, even—and I found myself riding better than I would have if I had just been pack filler.

I began feeling better, too, as the race wore on. It got to the point, in fact, where Roy continually asked me to slow down. I understood where he was coming from, but I was channeling my Tulip-green-clad self from the Tour de Suisse the year before. I wanted to ride everyone into the ground. It was a great feeling.

After I had spent a couple of days helping the Coors Light guys, Len asked me to come talk with him. I entered the hotel room and sat down with him and Alexi Grewal, another Coors star who had won the 1984 Olympic road race. They asked if I was available for the following season, meaning they wanted to hire me, full time, for the job I was doing for them in West

Virginia. For them, I'm sure it was all straightforward and normal. For me, it was surreal.

They said, "Are you free next year? Would you like to come ride for us?"

But I heard, "Would you like your death sentence overturned to come frolic in paradise?"

Moninger won the Tour of West Virginia, and I got a new lease on life.

Nineteen ninety-two marked my second trip to Philadelphia for the USPRO Championship. I really wasn't looking forward to it. When I had come to Philly the year before with the Tulip team, I had been overlooked by the media and out of shape. Despite the fact that my teammate Michel Zanoli won the event and another teammate, Adri van der Poel, finished fifth to add to our grip of cash, it was a very uncomfortable experience. I was a stranger in a familiar land, and it sucked.

When John Eustice asked if I would be willing to wear an earpiece and microphone in order to give in-race updates for the live television show, I was ecstatic. Now I had a purpose. Today, two-way communication between bike racers and team directors or the media is commonplace, but in 1992 it was cutting-edge. Maybe too cutting-edge because at the 1992 CoreStates USPRO Championship, it was a mess of cumbersome technology that didn't work very well. Basically I was wearing an earbud that was attached, by wire, to a receiver that was only slightly smaller than a shoebox. The transmitter consisted of a microphone that was clipped to my jersey, a wire, and another object that slightly resembled the first Walkman I ever saw. It had a bunch of knobs and dials that apparently did nothing—twist and turn as I might, nothing happened. I shoved all of this incredible technology into two of my three jersey pockets, leaving just one for the all-essential race food, and cut holes into the new jersey that I'd been saving for this particular race to allow a cleaner routing of the various wires. But even with all of this broadcasting equipment situated, no one could give me a clear answer as to when they were going to talk to me, if at all. Still, I was excited to have the assignment.

The race started, and I listened carefully for any instruction the commentators or show producers might be barking my way. I listened and listened. I turned the volume up and down. Several times I spoke into the microphone: "Check, check, check . . . hello . . . is this on?"

Nothing.

I listened to the sound of static and the voices of the commentators for as long as I could before finally yanking the earbud out and rejoining the race—for what it was worth. I honestly can't tell you who won or what else happened, but I can tell you that I was deaf in my right ear for about a week.

Back in Minnesota I began to feel sorry for myself and was angry that the form I had found in West Virginia was starting to rot. So when one of the brothers from the bike shop, Scott Flanders, called to invite me on a ride from Minneapolis to Duluth, I was suited up before the telephone call was even disconnected. Riding 180-plus miles in a day was exactly what I needed.

We launched at 5 A.M. from Minneapolis. We rolled out through the 'hood and headed toward the long and lonely road north. As soon as we got out of the city, a headwind kicked in, so we opted for a Trophy Baracchi—style attack on our ride, each of us exchanging turns at the front while the other tucked in tight behind and slightly to the side to escape the wind. Riding with Scott was easy because we both enjoyed about the same tempo, and neither of us was overly enamored with idle chitchat. After about a hundred miles, we stopped for lunch in Askov, where the vibe was strikingly akin to the café scene from *Easy Rider*. I felt as if all eyes in the place were burning holes in the back of my jersey. I wolfed down my food as fast as I could and hurried Scott to do the same. We paid the bill and got out of the café unscathed. Although the last 60-mile leg of our ride was definitely the most beautiful part of the journey, I was half expecting a clapped-out pickup truck with shotgun-wielding rednecks to show up at any minute, so I kept my eyes and ears open to avoid becoming a stain on the side of Highway 23.

Originally the plan was for us to ride to Duluth and hang out with Scott's in-laws for the weekend. Scott and his wife, Linda, would give me a ride back to Minneapolis Sunday evening, or I could take the bus. But with 180 miles of headwind behind me, I figured my best choice was to head back home by myself the following morning.

We woke up early, and Scott guided me out of town. Of course, as soon as he left me the wind started to pick up. It shifted from being the glorious anticipated tailwind to an evil, morale-killing headwind. I plodded along just fine until about 40 miles from home. That was when the wheels came off the wagon. Suddenly it wasn't possible for me to find a gear selection that worked; it was either too big or too small. It got to the point where the only thing I could get to work was a 53×14 at a ridiculously low cadence. I was also out of fuel, and my reserve tank was overdrawn. I had to stop at every convenience store I saw to buy another can of Coke and two-pack of Twinkies, doughnuts, or whatever other refined sugar product I could find. But after almost 11 hours and a half-million stops along the way, I found home.

Next on the Scott/BiKyle agenda was a little three-stage omnium in Cincinnati, Ohio, called Cyclebration. Stage one was a 1-kilometer uphill time trial, so we set out by bike to ride the 20 miles from our hotel to the start. As is often the case when planning a bike ride in an unfamiliar town, we picked the worst possible route. Road construction turned the four-lane road into a two-lane nightmare. On top of that, the start of the race was scheduled for late afternoon, which meant we were riding in rush hour, and people in cars were not all that pleased with us. Nevertheless, we kept ourselves in a single-file line as close to the right side of the road as we could. But that is never really enough.

"Get off the fucking road!" came a scream from the passenger-side backseat of a Ford Explorer. The voice was so hateful and the scream was so intense that I could smell what the man shouting it had eaten for lunch. I was the last one in our single-file line, so I took the brunt of the assault, and something snapped in me.

Without even thinking, I swung to the left and started to chase. I was in my biggest gear, mashing out as much hate as I could with every pedal stroke but brewing up as much hate as I was dispelling. I chased for a couple of miles until it seemed stupid to continue; with a 50 mph speed limit, they were gone. But just as I sat up, ready to throw in the towel, they caught a red light, so I put my head down again.

I rolled up to the SUV, ready to kill. The driver's wife saw me first and slunk down in the front passenger seat until I could no longer see her. The perpetrator of the assault, a very large man in the back, opened his window. I wanted to unleash a rabid soliloquy, but I was wrecked from the effort of the chase.

"What . . . were . . . you . . . thinking?" was all I could get out. I was hanging on to the doorpost by that point and was not about to let go without some form of satisfaction.

"Why the hell are you guys riding in road construction? You need to go ride somewhere else," the driver said.

"You think we did that on purpose, asshole?" I yelled. "We're not from here. We didn't know there would be construction. Don't fucking do that again."

I kept hanging on to the Explorer until I got an acknowledgment. When it came, though it lacked contrition, I let go and soft-pedaled until my teammates caught up with me. It must have been the warm-up I needed because I completely murdered the rest of the field in the prologue.

Stage two was a neat little circuit with a winding climb through a city park. There was no leader's jersey for me to wear, but leading this "stage race" was all the motivation I needed, and I rode away from everyone else to win in the best manner possible. When I crossed the finish line, there was no one else in the photo.

Since accumulated points instead of time determined the overall winner, the final stage was not a formality. I would need to work to defend my lead. But for the first time in my cycling career, the rest of the team rode for me. It was a role in which I was not completely comfortable, but it was interesting nonetheless. In an unexpected twist, former Milk Race champion Matt Eaton did the lion's share of the domestique work for me. In its day the Milk Race was an extremely important event on the elite amateur cycling calendar, a test that could almost be likened to a Tour de France proving ground. Had Matt refused to do any work to help me in this small race, I would not have been surprised. But he did, allowing me to go home with the overall victory even though I didn't collect the final stage win.

I had heard countless tales of Chequamegon since coming to Minnesota. The Chequamegon-Nicolet National Forest in northern Wisconsin is home to both the American Birkebeiner cross-country ski race and the Chequamegon Fat Tire 40, a 40-mile, point-to-point mountain bike race. Chequamegon is sometimes criticized by mountain bikers as not being a true mountain bike race—until, of course, they ride the event, when they find out just how devastating the varied and undulating terrain can be. In the previous two years Greg LeMond had made the race his own, and his presence had boosted the event's prestige immeasurably. LeMond had fallen sick and was skipping the 1992 race, but other fast guys, including Tom Schuler, had signed up.

Before the race I managed to pull together sponsorship from Gary Fisher Bicycles and RockShox, makers of the suspension forks. Hearing that there would be a lot of mostly dry dirt roads on the course this year, I had the tires pumped to almost 60 pounds per square inch of pressure. I lined up in the "preferred start" group just before the giant peloton of 1,600 riders rolled out of downtown Hayward behind a lead ATV. I stayed as close to the ATV as possible until we hit the first section of Birkie trail at a place called Rosie's Field. As soon as we were officially racing, I put my head down and went as hard as I could, hoping to eventually end up in the front group. As luck would have it, that group consisted of just three of us.

Locals Erik Ringsrud and Dewey Dickey had both spent time racing as elite-level amateurs in Europe, so I felt that I was in good company. Erik was also an accomplished mountain bike racer who had won a fair amount of races around the Midwest. We rode as if we'd made the decisive breakaway in one of the Classics; everything was smooth. The miles clicked past, and as I'd done so many times before, I counted my breakaway companions—one, two—and banked on finishing no worse than third.

But as we entered the final 3 miles of the race—a twisty section of double-track, complete with some short, steep climbs—my years of riding on the front, fighting with the wind, or simply holding on for dear life got the better of my breakaway companions, and I rode away from them. At the top of the last descent I could see the crowd gathered for the finish. Although they numbered in the hundreds, to me it was as good as if I were soloing in for victory in one of the Classics or the World Championships that I'd raced in Belgium; my eyes saw hundreds of thousands of spectators. I adjusted my jersey and saluted the crowd just as a great champion would.

2

PHILADELPHIA FLYER

NINETEEN NINETY-THREE DIDN'T EXACTLY START ON A HIGH NOTE. In fact, I would say that it was the worst season of my cycling career. After trading phone calls over the winter with Coors Light Cycling Team director Len Pettyjohn, it now seemed that any chance I had for a spot on his team was gone. Len already had a strong stage and classics rider in Roy Knickman, and I would have been filling essentially the same role. Instead Len added John Lieswyn, who, though only one year younger than I, was perhaps seen as having a brighter future.

All through the off-season I had counted on the Coors spot. It was a mistake that caught me off guard because also gone was any chance of a ride with the other powerhouse American team, Saturn. My fallback was a spot with Scott/BiKyle again, but I was hoping for something more national in scope. I looked into the possibility of riding mountain bikes. Bob Roll had made the change and was getting more press for it than he had in his days riding for the big 7-Eleven and Motorola teams in Europe. Unfortunately, though, the equipment, contingency, and money that I was able to put together to race mountain bikes paled in comparison with the offer I received from Scott/BiKyle, so I signed on for another season. The Philadelphia Flyers of the National Hockey League had upped their financial commitment to the team for '93, which meant we were to campaign a slightly larger race schedule and, more importantly, that I would be making $6,500 for the season—$2,000 more than the year before.

I had spent the winter of 1991–1992 riding my mountain bike on snowmobile trails when the weather was wretched and riding on the road whenever the temperature was above 25 degrees. Way back in high school I'd frozen a few body parts as a member of the cross-country ski team, but I had really done some damage riding my bike outdoors during that first winter back in Minnesota. I am not a cold-weather person, and the low temperatures took their toll. Throughout the winter of '92–'93, I made it outside only a few times, opting instead to stay indoors and ride the rollers. But my desire to make a name for myself as a cyclist in America had all but disappeared, and the rollers were as torturous and inhumane as a frontal lobotomy. The junkies I was hanging out with were infinitely more interesting than the hordes of American cyclists for whom racing was an excuse for training instead of the other way around.

At the same time that my inability to ride in the cold and my indifference toward the American road racing scene was making a mockery of my off-season fitness regimen, I was doing some construction work on a complete remodel of an old Minneapolis house and hitting the Twin Cities' good music scene at night. I don't think a week went by that I didn't see at least a couple of really good shows—shows in cramped, smoky bars that didn't start until after 11 P.M. at the earliest. Consequently, when I joined the guys for the first races of the season, my fitness was nowhere near where it had been at the same time the year before. A pro bike racer's job isn't guaranteed to be fun, but every minute of this new season was hateful.

We were sent off to Asheville, North Carolina, for training camp. North Carolina is beautiful country. When I was a kid my family had lived in Charlotte for 18 months. It was where I got my first real bike, a blue Schwinn Midget Stingray. But Asheville was completely foreign to all of us on the team. We mostly just stuck with the same ride every day, an out-and-back on the Blue Ridge Parkway.

An out-and-back is for the cyclist what a half pack of cigarettes is for someone who is trying to quit smoking—an excuse. "Oh, I'll quit as soon as I suck these last ones down." It was a little too easy to turn around sooner than we should have, and we definitely succumbed to the easier path. "Yeah, this is pretty good—we might not have a good place like this to turn around for the next 50 miles. We'll go farther tomorrow."

Asheville was also not so kind with its weather during our time there and offered up a heaping helping of cold, gusty winds and some rain. What should have been time spent beating ourselves up on the bike, followed by good meals and legs up in our hotel rooms, was replaced by excuses to turn around, fast food, trips to the mall to fend off the hotel-room boredom, and, for me at least, another beer. The Belgian-bred toughness had seemingly left my body.

Our tour of the South was to be capped off with the First Union Grand Prix in Atlanta. It was a 118-mile race of nine long laps and five short ones over a flat course, but even though I'd ridden okay in the same race the year before, I wasn't looking forward to it this time around. I knew my fitness was not there, so it would be a struggle. Cycling is funny like that; when you are riding well, you can hurt yourself completely, and *that* pain is okay because you feel like you are accomplishing something. When you're not riding well, the pain is a dull ache that you can neither make disappear nor elevate to any sort of positive outcome. It is like a crippling form of boredom or depression that you simply cannot escape.

We headed off toward Atlanta in our white Pontiac Transport clown-mobile van, loaded up with bikes and other crap. Also along for the ride was the second ferret in my collection, an albino I named Edith (after the late French singer Edith Piaf) that I had bought on one of our trips to the mall. It was my turn to drive, and I was making the best of the empty stretches of North Carolina road. I'd been keeping the speedometer needle nestled at around 95 mph for quite a while, but when the road flattened and straightened out so that we could see for miles ahead of us, I suddenly got a bad feeling and lifted my foot off the pedal. The needle dropped. And then I saw it: An unmarked but obvious police-type car was heading in the opposite direction and hit me with its radar. I couldn't be sure how fast I was going when he got me, but I was sure he'd be behind me pretty soon. I slowed to the 55 mph speed limit and waited for the lights. It didn't take very long.

I watched in the mirror as the North Carolina state trooper stepped out of his car, adjusted his Smokey the Bear hat, and began to walk toward me. He had been in the U.S. Marines. I was absolutely positive about that and would have laid money on a bet that he'd also been a drill instructor. My dad had been a drill instructor at the Paris Island Marine Corps Recruit Depot in South Carolina, and this guy had exactly the same walk and posture. I also noticed the Confederate flag sticker on the bottom of his clipboard.

"Great," I said to myself. "Here I am with long hair, an earring, red jeans, Dr. Martens boots, a Minnesota driver's license, Pennsylvania plates, the goofiest-looking vehicle on the road complete with a bunch of bikes on top, a car full of skinny guys, and an animal that looks like a stretch-limo rat. I am screwed."

The trooper told me he'd clocked me doing 78 mph, and since that was more than 15 miles over the speed limit, I would have to follow him to the nearest police station. He then took my license and told me to wait. After a few minutes the trooper returned, gave me back my license, and told me to follow him.

We arrived at the police station, where I was escorted into a waiting cell, though no bars or doors were closed. After a few minutes the trooper and the magistrate came into the cell. The magistrate was a cross between Hal Holbrook and Henry Fonda and was wearing a well-worn suit. His Honor held up a Bible and proceeded to swear in the trooper, who spent roughly three minutes explaining the details of the case. It was a completely bewildering feeling, to say the least, to stand in a jail cell in some tiny little burg just off the highway, having my immediate future decided by an old man and an ex-marine.

When the people had rested their case, so to speak, the magistrate looked at me with a sober yet somewhat empathetic expression.

"I am setting your bail at 150 dollars. Can you pay that?"

"Yes, sir, I can," I answered.

"I am setting your trial for three months from today," he added. "If you will not be present in court, you need to find an attorney to represent you."

I nodded in agreement.

"You need to understand that your bail is not your fine," he explained, perhaps sensing that I viewed 150 bucks as a pretty fair fine, especially considering what it could have been if the trooper had gotten me just a few miles earlier. "If you are not present and have no representation in court, you will lose your driving privileges in North Carolina, and you quite possibly will lose your license in your home state. Do you understand?"

"Yes, I do."

Of course I didn't fully understand why they needed me to come back with my organ-grinding monkey and open checkbook in three months, but I also didn't want to stay and chat anymore. With that I was led to a counter where I was processed and paid my bail. I then surrendered the keys to my teammates.

That little bit of fun in North Carolina eventually cost me $550.

I wish I could say that my speeding ticket foreshadowed being really fast at the First Union Grand Prix, but it was the opposite.

Lance Armstrong took off in a break with about 15 other guys and left the rest of us in the dust. The field eventually came together, and, surprisingly, Armstrong did not win—Malcolm Elliott slipped through at the end to take the victory—but I was garbage. I raced with all the excitement of a 55 mph speed limit, and none of my teammates even made the top 25. I couldn't wait to go home.

I called Northwest Airlines to double-check the rules for transporting a ferret back to Minnesota. I had done this before without trouble, but I thought I should make sure they hadn't suddenly decided to start charging thousands of dollars to transport pets. They hadn't, but the rules definitely had changed. My flight was for the next day, and in order for me to bring Edith along, she was going to need to visit the vet. While you can bring a cat on board, ferrets are strictly belowdecks animals. There would be no way for me to get her to a vet in time unless I visited a 24-hour emergency clinic or something. It was time for a different plan.

One of the best parts about having the Philadelphia Flyers hockey team as a Scott/BiKyle sponsor was that we all got a real, live, honest-to-goodness Flyers hockey jersey emblazoned with our name on the back. A hockey jersey is pretty close to worthless as a piece of clothing, but it was fun to be a part of the team, even if we were fourth cousins to the guys with the skates. The best part of the jersey with the name *Parkin* on the back was that it was big enough to hide something inside it—like a ferret that didn't have the proper paperwork to fly on Northwest Airlines.

I was staying at my teammate Dan Fox's parents' home, and Dan had agreed to drive me to the airport. I had a beat-up old

Adidas gym bag that was just big enough to carry my small pet carrier without looking too weird. I'd managed to pilfer a few First Union Grand Prix musette bags and figured that one of those would work perfectly for transporting my small pet through the security screening. This was, of course, well before 9/11, so as long as I didn't set off the metal detector, I was pretty much home free.

Dan and I arrived at the airport, and I put Edith in the musette and safety-pinned the top closed so she couldn't sneak out and cause widespread airport chaos. Ferrets typically sleep about 20 hours per day, so I hoped she would stay relatively still in the "sleeping bag" that I was carrying under my arm. Hope and reality don't always work hand in hand, though—Edith squirmed all through the check-in process. Of course, as soon as we were checked in, she went to sleep.

I hurried off to the security checkpoint, thinking this was my best and safest window of opportunity. As I approached the metal detector, she woke up. This time, instead of just being squirmy, she tried to chew, scratch, and muscle her way out of the bag. The extra-loose hockey jersey was dancing on my body of its own accord, and I knew there was no way I'd get through security like that.

I tried as hard as I could not to look panicky, made a quick U-turn, and headed for the bathroom. I hoped if people were looking at me, it would appear as if I simply remembered I had to pee. I went in, washed my hands very slowly, and went back outside. I found a bank of chairs that was out of view of the security checkpoint and sat down. After a few minutes Edith fell asleep. I stood up slowly, trying not to disturb her, and shuffled back to security as quickly as possible. There were a couple of people in front of me, just enough human traffic that the security officers didn't get a long look at me. I was hoping none of them were hockey fans who'd want to grill me on the Flyers' lousy season (they hadn't even made it into the playoffs). I threw my bag on the belt, waited for the signal, then walked through the metal detector. Goal! Safely through, Edith woke up. This time, though, I made my way to the bathroom and put her in the pet carrier, leaving the zipper on the gym bag ever so slightly open so that she could breathe. Luckily for us, the airplane was almost completely empty, so no one was any the wiser that I had a contraband animal on board.

Back in Minneapolis, I continued to train on the road, but I also raced my mountain bike. I had worked out a deal with the local Univega rep, Kurt Kempainnen, for two mountain bikes at his cost that I would campaign regionally for the season. I was starved for road competition and was hoping that doing some off-road racing could compensate. The dearth of road events was not because there weren't races going on but because so few of them were open to pros. USPRO, the governing body for professional cycling in the United States, and the USCF were completely separate entities at that point in America's cycling rebirth. There was a gap between the two classes because of this, making it hard (or at least confusing) for race promoters to open their races to pros as well as amateurs. I had been completely spoiled by the abundance of racing in Belgium and wanted to race as much as possible instead of spending my time plodding along on the endless, straight, flat, windy farm roads of southern Minnesota. But the race promoters weren't used to having pros want to compete in their races, so they hardly ever checked the box on the permit application that allowed them an "open class" race.

I did sneak into a few road races. It started with a Wednesday Night World Championship–type event at the Minnesota State Fairgrounds. The races themselves and the series overall were worth nothing but bragging rights, but it seems that bragging rights are stronger currency than actual cash in many cases, and the competitors began to protest against me after just one event.

This attitude mystified me. I remember racing the Twilight Criteriums in Northern California after I had moved there in 1985, where nothing in the world pleased me more than lining up next to the likes of Eric Heiden, Bob Roll, and the odd out-of-town star. For me, it was a learning experience; I could watch what they did and critique or admire it accordingly, though I remember having mostly admiration for these guys.

So whenever I was at home, which was most of the year, I would forsake the road bike for my mountain bike. I had a US-PRO racing license, and I was able to obtain a license from the off-road sanctioning body, the North American Off-Road Bicycle Association (NORBA), which also categorized me as a "pro" even if the boundaries between professional and amateur were more blurred in the off-road world.

The local mountain bike racers had perhaps even more disdain for me than the road bike racers, but I could get past that if for no other reason than because I could actually race my bike. Time and time again I was told that I lacked the skill to compete with these guys, even though I was finishing tens of minutes in front of them. It was as if winning races was not good enough because I had failed to "get rad" over some semicontrived obstacle instead of finding the fastest line through the section and pedaling faster on the climbs.

Despite the misguided cynics, there were still a few people with whom I could truly connect, as if they were secretly filled with Belgian blood too. Atop this list was Gene Oberpriller. Gene, or Geno, as he is known, is one of the most colorful characters I have ever met. He was born on February 29, which perhaps explains that while his driver's license may say one thing, he carries much of the innocence of someone one-fourth his age. To Geno, everything is interesting—fascinating, even. He was born with the physiology and bike-handling skills that could have taken him to the absolute top of the sport, but his interest in like-minded people, and all of the experiences life and bikes have to offer, brought him to a different path. I have often envied him for that.

Geno and I began to ride together more frequently and raced together as much as we could. Racing against each other was so much fun that we made a pact to split our pooled winnings straight down the middle every time we raced together. We never employed any "team tactics" against anyone, nor did we put on any sort of professional wrestling–type show. Our agreement was hatched simply so that we could race against each other for racing's sake and any financial rewards would be shared equally. We did okay too, because despite the presence of a young up-and-comer by the name of Jeff Hall, who was capable of putting us both in a world of hurt for at least a lap or two, Geno and I often walked away from a weekend of mountain bike racing with $600 or so to split.

After a short reprieve it was back to the road, so I packed my gear, bought a plane ticket, and headed to Philadelphia to meet up with the guys. Next on our agenda would be the crux of the Tour of America series. We'd start in Pittsburgh with the Thrift Drug Classic—one of the most brutal racecourses on the calendar—followed by the Tour of West Virginia, then go on to what most of us referred to as CoreStates week—Lancaster, Trenton, and the 156-mile USPRO Championship in Philly.

My form had yet to be found, but I was riding well enough to think I might be able to sneak into some early breakaway in Pittsburgh. Truthfully, I was hoping to ride myself into shape during the Tour of West Virginia, finding enough form there to then do something in Lancaster or Philadelphia. It would have been possible to do that had Pittsburgh been a European race, but we were racing in America, after all, so things were going to be different.

In Europe long races generally had frantic starts, somewhat calmer middle sections, and a furious finale. American racing, on the other hand, was frantic throughout. As a result, the speeds at the end of the race were most often a lot slower than those seen during the first half. It often seemed to me that the "athlete" part of the average American bike racer was quite a bit better than that of his European counterpart, but the "racer" part was much weaker.

We rolled out through the streets of Pittsburgh, and I, at least, was dreading the impending doom of the climb up Mount Washington. The climb is not that long, but given its ridiculously steep pitch, it is absolutely no fun at all. The peloton was nervous, but it was not the sort of nervousness I'd experienced in the World Championship Road Race in 1988, where I'd felt ready to either make something amazing happen or fail miserably. Here I felt the nervousness of a kid being called to the principal's office for some offense he knows he can't deny. I knew it was going to be unpleasant, I just didn't know exactly *how* unpleasant.

I don't know what lap we were on when it happened. My memory has been erased by the vision of that moment, as if I saw some brilliant light and heard the voice of a celestial being. All I can remember is that I was riding very close to the front of the peloton and was being protected by my Australian teammate, Tony Davis, when it happened: Lance Armstrong attacked.

"You gotta go with him," Tony urged.

"Fuck . . . *you* go with him," was my answer. Lance had just attacked with the fury of a Formula 1 car, and I felt like I was piloting a Geo Metro in dire need of a valve job.

I remembered, on several occasions when I had seen the Italian great and two-time world road champion Gianni Bugno attack, thinking that he possessed the most lethal nonsprint acceleration in the world. Watching Lance attack at the foot of the Mount Washington climb was at least doubly impressive. He disappeared from our ranks in a metaphorical burst of smoke and went on to win the Thrift Drug Classic decisively.

I dropped out of the race but was, nevertheless, a guest of the doping control, chosen yet again to pee in a cup. Since coming back to the States I had been making a visit to the doping control office at just about every race where they had one. I didn't mind being treated to the ice-cold drinks and conversing with the UCI officials, but the idea that I was being singled out again and again was moderately aggravating, especially since I knew that I was racing clean.

"What method do you guys use for picking the randoms?" I asked.

"We double-click a digital stopwatch and use the last two or three numbers," replied the official.

"That's interesting since I have been wearing the same number in these races for two years," I said facetiously. "Maybe I should buy a lottery ticket."

There was no response.

"You know," I started, "I really don't care if you guys pick me as random every time I race . . . I really don't. But perhaps you might want to make it first, second, and third places, plus two randoms and Joe."

There was no response.

We drove to West Virginia for the Kmart Tour of West Virginia. I was looking forward to the prologue time trial in Morgantown. The horseshoe-shaped course required enough bike-handling skill to make it interesting. Plus, I had always been a fan of the prologue time trial. As usual, we were housed in a dormitory for at least the first couple of nights and were on our own for food. After my various tours of the South and the Eastern Seaboard, I was hoping to find a restaurant that was a cut above the standard Cracker Barrel or Olive Garden. Since Morgantown is a college town, I ventured off in search of interesting victuals.

I came across a little hippie place called Mountain People, where the menu promised I could get something both healthy and tasty. I parked my bike outside where I could still see it and wandered in. I placed my order and sat down to wait, excited at the prospect of my first interesting meal in a long time. One of the other customers, whom I took to be a regular, had been speaking nonstop since I'd first walked into the place, but with only waiting for my food on my mind, I unfortunately started to hear what he was saying.

"So which one of our merry band, do you think, will represent us in this bike thing?" he asked in no particular direction.

After receiving answers in the form of shrugging shoulders and barely audible grunts, he directed his attention at me, the only Lycra-kitted patron anywhere near the Mountain People.

"Hey, you," he started, "are you here for this bike tour thing?"

Secretly I wanted to pull a pistol out from some secret, all-concealing jersey pocket and shoot this guy in the face. Instead I channeled my dad.

"Yes, sir, I am. Beautiful country here."

He continued to wonder aloud which locals would be represented. He then shifted his attention toward one of the other customers.

"Hey, Benny," he barked, "you should join this thing. You ride your bike all the time."

The guy then turned back to me.

"Hey, where do you sign up for this tour?" he asked.

"Well," I said carefully, "this is an invitation-only race . . . one that's open to professionals and a few amateur national teams only." I shrugged.

"So how many professional women are there?" he said.

"You know, I don't really know. There aren't any here, though."

"Why not?" he asked, as if looking for a fight. "Are you scared they're going to beat you? Would that embarrass you?"

"No—"

"That's awfully sexist, now, isn't it?" he interrupted.

"Listen," I answered, glaring and pointing, "this is not about *that*. This is bike racing . . . elite-level bike racing. There is not a woman I know of who would be dumb enough to come and get her ass kicked here. It is a muscular, physical, and hormonal thing that has nothing at all to do with any sort of equal rights."

"Hormones . . . like testosterone? Are you even tested for steroids?" he asked, confusing the subject. "No wonder you don't allow women!"

"Yeah, we are. But fuck you," I replied. "Fuckin' hippies." I turned my back on the guy and walked out. I'd been in West Virginia less than 24 hours, and I was already done with it.

I pre-rode the prologue course until I felt comfortable with all but one of its six turns. Despite my run-in with one of Morgantown's more close-minded citizens the day before, I thought I might be able to make it onto page one of the results sheet.

I had spotted a coffeehouse on the start straight of the race-course and asked our adjutant director to come with me to grab a cup. Since the course had us racing the wrong way on one-way streets and everything was closed to all vehicles but race traffic, I thought it wouldn't be a problem to ignore the signs forbidding bicycles on the sidewalk. I was wrong.

As Mark and I made our way up the sidewalk toward the cof-feehouse, an old man took offense at what he apparently viewed as my scofflaw attitude and started screaming, *"Get. That. God. Damned. Bi-cycle. Off. The. God. Damned. Sidewalk!"*

He came at me with all the speed and fury that an old man could muster, smacked me across the back with his cane, and then stuffed it into the spokes of my front wheel. In his eyes I could see nothing but hatred—hatred toward me, this race, and life itself. In the old man's glare I also imagined that I could see my dad's eyes and the confusion that lived inside his brain when Alzheimer's set in. Despite that sensation, I became the ugly visi-tor, spewing obscenities at the top of my lungs. I pushed the old man back with no regard for his age, his dignity, or his physical or mental condition. Had he swung at me, I would have come back with the full anger of a frustrated and homesick skinny guy.

A year earlier, when I had been verbally assaulted by a big guy in the backseat of a Ford Explorer, the experience had generated just enough rage to launch me into a prologue time trial victory and the eventual overall victory of a small stage race in Cincin-nati. This run-in, though, took any remaining wind out of my sails. I sucked in the prologue and proceeded to stink up the joint for the rest of the Tour of West-by-God Virginia. Not allowing himself to be bothered by hippies or old men, Lance Armstrong went on to put the race in his pocket.

———

CoreStates week was a trifecta that started with an 86-mile circuit race in Lancaster, moved on to a 90-mile circuit race in Trenton, and finished with the richest one-day race in America,

the USPRO Championship in Philadelphia. I had been looking forward to it, thinking I could maybe pull off a top five in
Lancaster or Trenton. I knew I'd ridden myself into some sort
of form in West Virginia, but given my current state of funk, I
didn't have high hopes. Add to that the fact that my teammates
and I were about ready to kill our Polish teammate, Jerzy Wozniak, and feed his body to hogs somewhere in Bucks County. The
situation had been escalating since we'd first spent time with
the guy. Although we were a shit-kicker team with little hope
of doing much of anything, anywhere, our core group had come
together pretty well and did what it could. If Tom Armstrong or
Tony Davis found himself in a breakaway that looked like it might
end up in a bunch sprint, Dan Fox and I would do everything we
could to help. When any of the other mercenaries, such as Matt
Eaton or Steve Tilford, joined our squad, they worked together
with us. We were a team. Wozniak either thought himself too
good for us or was too dumb or too complacent to care.

After a lackluster team performance in Lancaster, a course
that was almost purpose-built for a rider like me, my frustration
level with Wozniak had reached a boiling point, and the rest of
the guys weren't far behind me. I wanted him gone. I called Kyle
at his home and gave him the business. While I believe to this
day that I had a valid argument, I presented it as rationally as if
I were a spoiled six-year-old who didn't get the pony he'd asked
Santa Claus to bring him for Christmas. Kyle was having none
of it and nearly hung up on me.

So we set out for Trenton for our last tune-up before the big
throw-down in Philly. Trenton's flat and fast course, under the
attack of so many good national and international professionals,

made it a lot of fun to ride, but it was also one of the harder races for a nonsprinter like me to collect any sort of decent result.

Through the first half of the race it looked even less promising for my teammates and me. I was spending half of my effort paying attention to the race and the other half paying attention to what Wozniak was doing. I was determined to chase down any move of value that he might find himself making, but as the race wore on I began to see that he had no real chance for any sort of result.

The race in Trenton, like the one in Lancaster, was a lap race—a kermis, for lack of a better word to describe it. There were no *frites* stands or carnival games, and most definitely no dried fish, but it was the sort of race I had become good at while living in Belgium. Almost as if the race organizers wanted to give me a little gift, there was a section of cobblestones. As our giant peloton warped through the streets of Trenton, I found myself feeling a little bit like a European pro again. It was easy for me to keep myself at the front, and though I knew I would eventually find myself being shuffled to the back in order to avoid the inevitable sprint finish of more than a hundred lunatics, I no longer cared. I was quite certain that this would be my last year making my living (bleak as it was) on two wheels, so I was practically celebrating every pedal stroke.

Small attacks were going off left and right and began to include some of the more important riders in the race. I saw Phil Anderson, the Aussie pro who was riding for Armstrong's Motorola squad. I saw Roberto Gaggioli, an Italian who had won USPRO Philly in 1988 and had been picked up by Coors Light. And I saw a rider in a Mercatone Uno jersey flash by. I figured I should play along. These were good wheels to follow. I was already near the front of a fast-moving peloton, so I stood up on a big gear and sneaked off to join the as-yet unformed group. We came together and immediately began working to stay away. That is the biggest difference between the pro ranks and the amateurs; when a small group of pros tries to break away, little or no conversation is exchanged at the start of the attempt. If a rider is too weak to do his fair share, he'll stay out of the way until he either recovers from the effort that got him there or he's eventually dropped. Very rarely will that rider receive any verbal attacks from his breakaway partners. That's the way it was working here. Other than the occasional call-out to let one of the others know someone was going to miss his turn at the front, no one in our group was saying a word.

Since Gaggioli was one of Coors Light's toughest sprinters and Phil Anderson was one of Motorola's superstars, I knew both of their teams were content to let this little group go. With those teams sitting idly by, there were no other teams in the race with the ability to chase like they'd need to. There was plenty of horsepower behind us but none of the organization needed to get the job done.

As we started the last lap, it looked likely that our group of four would be contesting the win. As we climbed the small hill and entered the park at the far end of the course, it was all but certain. We raced through the park fairly flat-out, descended the hill again, and then aimed for the finish line. Gaggioli and Anderson watched each other closely enough that Phil's attacks seemed more show-like than meant to hurt anyone. The rider from Mercatone Uno, Angelo Canzonieri, was watching the other two just as I was. With about a kilometer and a half to go before the line, Phil and Roberto swung off to the left and sat up, and

Canzonieri mounted a somewhat anemic attack. I kept watching the two stars. It was a bit of a gamble, but I was hoping to be able to attack closer to the line.

Sure enough, they decided it was far enough out from the line that they could still recover from one more effort before the final sprint, so they chased the Mercatone Uno rider down. I slotted in behind them. As we caught Canzonieri, I started thinking, which is sometimes the worst thing a rider can do. As my old soigneur, Fons von Heel, used to say, "If you start to wonder if this is the moment to attack or not, you're already too late." My moment of hesitation cost me the race. Had I attacked as hard as I could have at the very moment that the tempo began to slow, the two main men in the breakaway might possibly have hesitated for a brief second too, and I might have made it to the line first.

They sprinted in, and I rode in just behind them. Though I probably should have been dejected, I was fairly content with what I had just accomplished. More importantly, I had been able to feel like an honest-to-goodness bike racer again, if only for a little while. Three days later, though, I was back in a funk, so the USPRO Championship came and went with absolutely nothing to write home about. I rolled across the line in Philly a dejected 33rd in the company of my teammates Dan Fox, Mark Southard, and Steve Tilford.

The final stop for the Tour of America series in '93 was a brand-new race that was going to be held in my hometown of Minneapolis. Since I was the only local pro besides Greg LeMond, I was asked to speak at the official Norwest Cup press conference.

It was an event that was amazingly contrived but interesting nonetheless. The two bike racers who were representing the event were Bob Mionske and I. The CEO of Norwest Banks was present as well as the lieutenant governor of the state of Minnesota.

In addition to announcing the race, we were also announcing (and making a big deal out of) the Recycle a Cycle program that was running in conjunction with the race. Under this program people could take their old, worn-out bikes to local bike shops and Norwest branches. The bikes would be fixed up and given away to deserving kids at Norwest branches all over the Twin Cities area.

We all saddled up at the police station to pedal over to the Norwest building. Mionske, a former national champion and two-time Olympian, was now with the Saturn team and wore their colors. I was outfitted in my team clothing, the police were in their uniforms, and the corporate honchos pulled giant t-shirts over their dress shirts. We helped them fasten the straps of their ill-fitting helmets, then proceeded to ride the few blocks to Norwest headquarters. It was a fine parade.

Once inside the building, we made our way to the elevators and ascended to the top floor for the press conference. I had not thought much about what I would say. I listened to all of the big-wigs speak. I listened to Mionske speak. I listened as the course was described and the Recycle a Cycle program was announced. When it was my turn to talk I stepped up to the podium, thanked my riding partners for the chance to pedal with them, thanked the city of Minneapolis and Norwest Banks for hosting the race, and then told a story. I talked about how professional bike racers spend their lives racing in front of fans all over the country and the world, but most often we do it in places that are not even remotely close to our own hometowns. I told them that when, every once in a while, a race of this magnitude comes along in a rider's own backyard, it is incredibly motivating—it's like a home game taken to a whole new level.

It was no Gettysburg address, but it was one of the best little speeches I had ever given, and I was happy with it. I became an official spokesman for the event and even landed myself a spot in the race program as one of the riders to watch. In fact, my profile was positioned *above* Lance Armstrong's.

The Norwest Cup weekend was to be a busy one. First I needed to defend my Chequamegon Fat Tire 40 title on Saturday. Then there was the Norwest Cup on Sunday. My mom came to town to watch the first bike race she'd seen in a few years. We loaded up the car and made the three-hour drive from Minneapolis to Hayward, Wisconsin. Northwestern Wisconsin is very beautiful in the fall, but just as in Minnesota, the weather can go from decent to terrible in a hurry. It was the first time I would wear the number-1 plate on my bike, and I was more than anxious to defend it. I hadn't prepared as well for the '93 edition as I had the year before, but I still thought I had what it would take to make it to the top step of the podium.

Rolling out of town, I took my place behind the lead ATV and did my best impersonation of a *keirin* rider, sweeping back and forth to keep anyone from taking my spot. With no one but the quad in front of me, I was also able to ride without fear of someone grabbing a handful of brakes and taking me down. We rolled out Highway 77, and the pack grew more nervous. Then, about a quarter mile or so from the entrance to Rosie's Field, the quad driver upped the pace. I hung on as long as I could, but when he raised the speed one more time to shake me loose, I knew the race had begun.

Just as in one of the classics, albeit at a slower pace, we made a mad dash for the field. I recognized Rosie's from the year before but forgot just how long this first section of pain and suffering was going to be. With roughly 2,000 people all wanting to win Chequamegon, I knew that the best course of action would be what we'd done the year before, so I put my head down and went as hard as I could, more or less, until I was reasonably certain our little group was clear.

It was no surprise to me that Geno Oberpriller was with us. Also in the group was Dewey Dickey, who'd finished second the previous year. Rounding out our foursome was a Trek factory rider, Travis Brown. As the race's title sponsor, Trek had sent the mountain bike star to Chequamegon not only to represent the Wisconsin-based company but also to try to bring home the trophy.

The four of us rolled along nicely together, with Geno and me doing the lion's share of the work and Travis doing what he should have been doing, riding conservatively and watching the locals. Dewey seemed to be hurting a bit and was doing what he could to help the pace but definitely didn't seem to be a factor for the win.

As the race wore on, both Geno and I started to tire of our companions' pace; I think Geno was more tired of it than I was. He started rolling through a bit harder than he needed to and would open up little gaps that needed to be closed by one of us. I didn't know if he was doing it intentionally or not, so the first couple of times that a gap formed, I closed it, thinking perhaps Travis didn't know what else to do and Dewey was blowing up. But the gaps kept forming, so I sat up and watched my friend roll away from us. As easily as that, Geno was gone; he pedaled away like we were glued to the ground. The next time we saw him, he was standing on the top step of the podium. I know I should have tried harder for a podium spot myself, but with the win out of reach, I opted to limit my losses. Soft-pedaling, so to speak, I finished 4th so I might be able to do something on the streets of Minneapolis the following day.

The first Norwest Cup bicycle race in Minneapolis was pretty special. Thousands of fans lined the streets. It seemed to me as if this race was almost like a classic in terms of its number of spectators, which made the experience of racing in my hometown that much better. I was feeling pretty good right from the start, which was almost strange, given the 40 miles of mountain bike racing in my legs from the day before. I figured if I was feeling that good at the start, there was a strong possibility that I would be feeling even better toward the end of the race.

The course that was used for the '93 race contained a stretch of cobblestones just across the Hennepin Avenue Bridge from downtown. The cobblestones are fairly old and not unlike many sections of stones in Belgium, so it was fun to watch some of the riders struggle with them and even more fun to hear them compare the short stretch with something from Paris-Roubaix.

But the little slice of Belgium wasn't smiling back at me, and after just a few laps, I flatted my front tire. I threw my hand up immediately and began making my way to the back of the long peloton. We turned left at the end of the cobblestone section and climbed a short, block-long hill before making another left.

Since team cars were already passing me, I decided to jump off my bike and remove the front wheel so I'd be ready for the replacement as soon as the car got to me. The spot I'd chosen also allowed for our team car to stop and the mechanic to service me without blocking traffic.

Since time has a way of slowing down in situations like these, it seemed like forever before I spotted the Scott/BiKyle team car. As it made its way up the hill, I raised the wheel over my head and began waving. The people in the car had a radio and would have been informed that I needed assistance, but it's always a good idea to make oneself as big and visible as possible. They got closer, so I lowered my arm and tossed the flatted wheel over toward the crowd-control barriers that were keeping people and traffic off the course. When I looked back in the direction of the team car, expecting to see the door opening and our mechanic jumping out, wheel in hand, I saw that no one in the vehicle had seen me. They drove right past and were gone.

Instantly I flashed back to the 1988 World Championship, where a front flat and lack of a properly working radio had dashed any hope of a finish, let alone a good finish. In 1988 I had been riding really, really well, and I believe, with all my heart and mind, that I would have finished that race strong. Here in Minneapolis, I knew I would have finished. Maybe it wouldn't have been anywhere close to the podium and maybe it wouldn't have been strong, but I would have finished. I honestly believed that was to be the last time I ever would race bikes for a living, so I wanted to at least ride across the finish line instead of watching the finish on TV. I was too mad to speak and too sad to cry. I threw my bike.

3

SILVER BULLET

IT WAS THE FALL OF 1993, AND MY BIKE RACING CAREER WAS OVER. I had returned to the United States two years earlier with high hopes of making a name for myself in my home country, but I had failed to accomplish that goal. It was coming up on winter, and my hours in the bike shop were starting to taper off; I had to think about getting another job. For the past two years my total income had been only slightly higher than the $4,500 and $6,500 I'd been given by the team, so I was broke and lacked a plan. I was a bit like a turtle that's been flipped over on its back—confused and moderately helpless.

The bicycling season in Minnesota had come and gone, and so had any full-time hours at bike shops that didn't also cater to winter sports such as cross-country skiing. Since doing the remodel on a 1906 house where I lived, I'd become interested in carpentry, woodworking, and tools. I started kicking around a place called the Woodworkers' Store and within a few weeks was working part time selling hardware, tools, exotic hardwoods, and finishes in order to complement my part-time work at the Flanders Brothers bike shop. I think if I had gone straight into this job after returning from Belgium I would quite possibly have gone insane, perhaps even packed my bags and gone back to Belgium to find work as a mechanic on one of the teams if I couldn't beg my way onto a kermis team as a rider.

I had absolutely no idea what I was doing. The store specialized in European drawer and cabinet hardware, which is application-specific and somewhat technical—things that have never interested me. On Saturdays and Sundays the store was filled with DIYers wanting to replace hinges for which they had absolutely no reference. Since I was equally unprepared, we'd reach an impasse quickly, and the customer would either continue to stare cluelessly at the bins filled with cabinet-door hardware or ask me just what the hell I was doing working there.

I learned to hang out in the basement, where the wood was kept, so I could help the people who were actually planning on making something. Most of these folks had a bit of a clue, so all I had to do was point out where the type of wood they were looking for was located and then, in most cases, cut a length of it for them.

Working at the Woodworkers' Store was a rough shock to my system. Since all of the other people working there were expert in some form of woodworking, I felt like the token idiot a lot of the time. But working at the bike shop was not that much better. I'd learned how to work on bikes from a Euro race mechanic, meaning I could make a bike clean, wrap handlebars, and glue on a tire like a champ. Just about everything else was beyond my ability. Add to that the fact that most high-end road bike customers came in prepared to argue the virtues of different types of steel tubing but had absolutely no clue when it came to frame geometry and bike fit, and it became a recipe for disaster.

These road bike customers would always begin with the phrase "I've been reading about . . ." and quickly go on to explain that based upon their riding style, they thought they should find a frame made out of this or that tubing brand's XYZ tube set. This, of course, was at a time when there were limited choices for frame materials. There were some top-end racing bikes with aluminum tubing, and carbon-fiber composites were starting to get more play. Titanium was making a splash, but it was so costly that few riders could afford it. Apart from these exotics, the frames most people were buying and riding were almost all the same, differentiated primarily by their fit and finish, their geometry, and a half-dozen or so kinds of steel tubing. The problem was that, aside from the paint job, most people could not tell the difference, especially those who had just started riding a road bike. I knew my days for bike shop employment were numbered the first time I called out a customer on this simple fact.

"Sir, how long have you been riding road bikes?" I asked.

"I started riding in June," came the reply.

"Well, then, the best thing for you to do is look up on that wall behind me." I pointed. "Find the frame you like the most, color-wise and graphics-wise. We will then look at the size and geometry and figure out if we need to order you one or if you can ride the one we have in stock."

His look told me he was not impressed.

"I'm not trying to be a jerk, but you're not going to feel the difference between Columbus SL and SLX," I continued, ticking off the names of two of the most popular types of Italian steel tubing. "I've ridden it all, and I can hardly tell. I can tell you the difference between steel, aluminum, and carbon fiber—and I have been a pro bike racer for seven years—but the steel stuff is pretty subtle. You'd be better advised to spend your time talking about components and shoes and pedals. Then we can get you all set up so that your position is perfect."

He asked to talk with one of the Flanders brothers.

In December I got a call from Len Pettyjohn, the director for the Coors Light Team, telling me there was a space on the team for me if I wanted it. The call came without warning, and I had a hard time forming any intelligent sounds in response. Roy Knickman had decided to call it a career, leaving a hole in the roster that Len felt would be nicely filled by someone like me. The dollar amount was $35,000, and Len apologized that it could not be more. I didn't care; I just wanted the job. I wanted to race my bike again, but with a bigger team. I wanted a purpose other than just filling out the peloton. It was one of those moments when I felt as if the weight of the world was being lifted off my shoulders.

I had to have my contract faxed to the coffee shop across the street because the bike shop didn't have a fax machine, and I didn't either. It didn't take long to run through the details. I signed the document and sent it back to Len's office right away.

I was working about 30 hours per week at the Woodworkers' Store and about 20 at the Flanders Brothers. Apart from the 2-mile round trip to and from both jobs, I wasn't riding my bike at all, so I decided I'd better quit one of them and get on with some kind of search for fitness. It wasn't hard to decide between hanging out in a bike shop for a few more weeks or helping pissed-off weekend carpenters find obscure cabinet hardware. I met with Steve, the manager of the Woodworkers' Store, and told him about the offer I'd gotten to ride for Coors Light. I told him the opportunity was one of a lifetime, and the dollar amount on the table was so good it was almost *obscene*, which, compared to what I'd been making, wasn't far from the truth. Two weeks later I officially became an ex-employee.

Shortly after the new year began I headed to Northern California to train on some of the roads I had ridden as a USCF junior before I had left for Belgium. I loved those roads and knew I would be able to find at least some decent base fitness there. My indoor-trainer regimen wasn't doing the job, and I simply couldn't show up to training camp as a worthless sack of unfit garbage. Unfortunately, though, the way I attacked the NorCal roads was quite a bit different than the way I had trained as a junior. In those days I had mostly rolled along in a small gear, opting for an even smaller one when the road went uphill. Now, as an aged veteran of pro cycling, I was used to a much bigger gear, so although I was technically traveling faster on my bike, my legs felt sluggish as my brain tried to trick me into thinking I was going slower than I had nine years earlier. I feared I was going to come up short when I got to the team training camp.

The Coors Light Team's camp was held in Santa Rosa, California. It was unlike any camp I had experienced when I was racing in Europe, and the training rides were also unlike any I'd been on before. Instead of the hard-core ritual of an entire massive team riding in close quarters, the 10 members of the Coors team were pretty much on their own programs. We did venture out for some group rides, but the rigid structure I'd become used to in Europe was completely absent. I guess I wasn't surprised by the relaxed nature of the squad, but I had thought we would act more like a single entity than we did.

Still, I was happy to be part of the powerhouse team and felt like I was getting along pretty well with the guys. By this point I knew all of them, either from racing as a junior in Northern California, from racing in Europe, or just from the previous two years of racing in America. Although we operated as a pretty cohesive unit, there were definitely camps within the 10-man squad. Since half of the guys lived in or around Boulder, Colorado, and the team was technically based there, the Colorado contingent was the most prevalent. I felt more at home with the Northern Californians on the team—Scott McKinley, Chris Huber, and our Italian Northern California teammate, Roberto Gaggioli, since they were a bit more rough-and-tumble. These three were our best sprinter types too, meaning they benefited more visibly from my domestique work than did the others. Even with a common language and friendly teammates, I'd always been more of a blue-collar bike racer, so I felt most at home hanging out with the mechanics and soigneurs.

Our first race of the season was to be a local NorCal event. I was excited to get back to work, and doing a race that was promoted by Velo Promo made me feel as if I were at home for the first time since I'd left Belgium. As a junior I had done quite a few of Bob Liebold's Velo Promo races, so the low-key event combined with a bit of nostalgia served to calm my fear of revealing that I was woefully out of condition.

Early-season races are always nerve-racking, whether you are racing a semiclassic in Belgium or a local event in California. So I decided that as a safety measure, and as a show of force, I would set tempo on the front as I had in 1991, when my Tulip teammate Luc Roosen had won the Tour de Suisse. After all, I had been hired largely to replace Knickman, who had been the Coors team's go-to domestique and tempo-setter for several years.

After the early-race attacks died down, I assumed my position at the front of the massive, nervous group and began to plod along in a big gear, making it easier for my teammates and other fit, experienced members of the peloton to shelter themselves from the wind. With the tempo lifted, the attacks seemed less severe as well, so the guys on my team had a chance to do something big toward the end of the race.

My teammate Scott Moninger was the first to approach me, letting me know that no one expected me to ride tempo all day long. Riding tempo this way is usually reserved for defending a leader's jersey in stage races or keeping the race together for a big sprint finish, but I wanted to mark my territory early. I wanted people to look at me as some sort of rabid old domestique, like a dog that will only let go of something it has in its mouth if you kill it.

I kept up the tempo, watching my legs as they became redder and more swollen with each pedal stroke—evidence of my serious lack of form—until finally a small group containing Moninger broke away. Moninger, the most intelligent and tactically savvy American-based bike racer I have ever seen, won easily. It was a small race but a fun way to start a season.

On our way to the hotel, Len reminded me that it was not my job to set tempo in races like this.

"I know," I answered. "I just felt like lifting my leg a bit."

"That's what I figured." He sniggered.

I had liked Len Pettyjohn from the first time I'd met him. He exuded the kind of confidence you see in race-car drivers and fighter pilots, a cockiness that is backed by skill and intelligence. He even looked like an adventurer, with a tall, thin frame and clear eyes that missed nothing. I saw in Len the same kind of skill in determining how to motivate different individuals that my old boss, José de Cauwer, possessed. Both directors also had the ability to make their riders feel like they would back us no matter what. Len was clearly better educated than the Belgian, though, so the way he handled things seemed, in many ways, calmer and more calculated.

The next big test for us was the Redlands Classic, held on the sunny roads of Southern California's inland empire. This stage race was surely going to prove to be too much for my fitness, but I was looking forward to getting some longer race miles into my legs. Sure enough, I struggled every time the road went up for any extended period, and I seemed to be lacking power and snap everywhere else. I felt like I was in a semiconscious haze and couldn't quite wake up. It was in Redlands that I first heard that Len would be receiving résumés from riders who had beaten me and other members of the team. Sure enough, shortly after the Redlands Classic, a résumé arrived at the Coors Light Team office in which a rider made specific note of finishing in front of me. The proud rider still hadn't cracked the top 50, though.

As the spring wore on, my fitness improved and I was awarded a spot on the squad that would be going to the Tour DuPont. For the past two years I had ignored the Tour DuPont as much as I could, feeling slighted for not being on a team that was in it. DuPont was a big-money stage race that attracted several European teams and all the top domestic squads, including the

American Motorola team led by Lance Armstrong, and I figured there wouldn't be much for me to do there except look out for my team leaders and bring bottles to the guys. Actually, I wasn't holding my breath for a podium finish for any of my teammates.

Nevertheless, I was excited to race in a highly talented pro peloton again. I was hoping that with a field of strong riders, the stages would play themselves out more as they did in Europe, with higher overall speeds and fewer nuisance attacks than I'd seen in most of the pro American races I'd been in. I was also looking forward to seeing some of the Dutch and Belgian riders I had ridden with.

Perhaps it was the presence of the Europeans or of my former soigneur Fons von Heel, or maybe that my former Tulip team-mate Adri van der Poel was there, but even with minimal form I felt pretty good—even a bit cocky—and though my results and our overall team presence were not anything to write home about, this Tour DuPont gave me some of my last truly inspired moments on a road bike.

Stage one looked likely to end up as a day for the sprinters, so I stuck close to Scott McKinley. Scott and I had raced against each other as juniors and again in Europe when he was riding for the 7-Eleven team. He was one of the best bike handlers and craftiest sprinters I have ever seen, so I wanted to make sure he got to the finish line with a chance to look for a great result.

When we hit the first and only climb of the stage, at least half of the riders in the field, McKinley included, found themselves in a bit of difficulty. For some reason I was completely calm and having no problem with the pace. I paced Scott as carefully as I could over the top of the climb, and then the two of us wove our way through traffic down the short descent. A gap had opened that left us in a second group. I was surprised to see no one making any effort to close the gap, so I went ahead and closed it. It was one of those magic moments where you can't even feel the pedals. Then, with less than 5 km to go, Scott flatted. I stopped and gave him my wheel so he could get back in the peloton right away instead of waiting for the team car to deliver a replacement. The exchange was quick, and he made it back to the front in time to sprint, but the effort left him just a bit short.

The Tour DuPont also allowed me to resume my role carrying water bottles from the team car to my teammates. Although this is far from glamorous work, I always had a good time seeing how many bottles I could stuff inside my jersey. It was also a lot of fun to weave through the cars and push other riders out of the way as I made my way back to the front of the race.

On one particularly fast and windy descent, I rode up to Scott Moninger and offered him a drink.

"Coke," he said. I obliged with a can. "I'd rather have it in a bottle," he said, handing me an empty water bottle. I'd never known a rider to prefer Coke in a bottle before. Since my very first in-competition Coke, the bottom half of a can that Dutch legend Joop Zoetemelk handed me as we were beginning the full finale of the semiclassic Veenendaal-Veenendaal, I'd always enjoyed the full carbonated power of this soft drink. In fact, the ritual of opening the can, drinking as much as you possibly could, and then passing it to another rider signaled the last few seconds of reprieve before the real attacking of the last 20 km began. But okay, if that was what Moninger wanted, that was what he would get.

I sat up, opened the Coke, popped open the water bottle, and emptied the can into it. We were rolling at nearly 50 mph, and since my hands were nowhere near the handlebars, just about any touch of brakes by riders in front of me would have been ugly.

"Oh shit. Oh shit. Oh shit. Oh shit" came out of the mouth of the rider on my left.

I stuffed the empty can into my jersey pocket, closed the bottle, and handed it back to Moninger, who chuckled, thanked me, and took a big drink. All I had done was pour Coke into a water bottle, but I was as giddy as if I had just won the World Championships.

In every stage race, riders start to count down toward the last day almost from the moment they climb the prologue start ramp. As the days continue, the nervousness begins to dissipate until the end is in sight, which is when the playful cockiness begins. Before the start of the stage one morning, I happened to approach the line along with Greg LeMond. The announcer, Phil Liggett, saw us, and after reminding the crowd of Greg's palmarès took the opportunity to talk about the two of us being fellow Minnesotans. Greg, who had moved himself in front of me, started lunging his back wheel backward, hitting my front wheel. Over and over he bumped my front wheel, and the two of us giggled like a couple of idiots. I quickly figured out that Greg had developed a rhythm to his attacks, so I timed one perfectly and threw my front wheel forward at the very moment he jerked his back at me. Somehow I caught him perfectly off guard and off balance, and before either of us knew what was happening, the two-time world champion and three-time Tour de France champ was on the ground, feet still connected to the pedals.

The Tour DuPont was promoted very well, and the mainstream press was there to report on the race. Perhaps in an attempt to take some of the spotlight and pressure away from our team leaders, Len directed attention toward me. I was interviewed, photographed, and interviewed some more; eventually I ended up with a photo and story in the newspaper *USA Today*. It was the first time in a long while that I'd gotten any press and was the only time I ever made a national newspaper in the United States. As we left the start on the morning that my story came out, Lance Armstrong offered his congratulations for the article; he was the only one to do so.

I was making it through the Tour DuPont without too much difficulty and even started feeling as if I might have the form to ride well within the next weeks. I decided that since the red rubber skinsuit I had worn in the prologue had helped me get into *USA Today*, I should wear it again for the final time trial. Within the team we often joked that if you aren't going to ride fast, you might as well look fast.

None of the team cars was going to follow me, and that was okay by me. I had grown used to that after José de Cauwer told me I was too anxious about time trials so he would no longer allow any of the team cars to follow me in the race of truth. After wrestling myself into the rubber suit, I climbed onto the start ramp and waited for the clock to tick down to start. I launched and quickly found a good gear. It seemed like I might be going too fast when I caught the first guy in front of me so soon, but I was feeling good, so I kept rolling. Ultimately I caught a few riders and started to feel fairly motivated. The course was good for me, flat and fast, so I could just push the big gear as hard as I could without worrying about transitioning on hills. The closer I got to the finish the more I started to feel like I was absolutely hauling ass, like this could be the ride that would get my name onto the first page of results.

With less than 5 km to go I passed one more rider, and then it happened . . . the rubber skinsuit attacked me. I'm not sure if it was the combination of heat and humidity—it was in the low 80s—or simply the constrictive nature of the suit for a distance that was well beyond that of a prologue, but I cracked. While I have had my fair share of meeting the man with the hammer—bonking, cracking, whatever you want to call it—this was more of a panic attack than anything I have ever felt, before or since. I sat up and tore at the zipper for all my feeble body was worth. I finally got the thing open a little bit, but only after getting passed by a couple of the guys I had so handily caught earlier. The strange attack seemed to take its toll on my legs too, because they gave up their ability to push over the huge gear.

When I finally limped across the finish line, all the riders I had passed had managed to pass me back. As I coasted to the team car, my old teammate Adri caught sight of me and started pointing and laughing. I'd managed to sweat out enough water that the rubber skinsuit was flapping on my upper body like a trash bag. Later that evening, after I found myself on the fourth page of results, I noticed that one of the guys I'd passed was on the first page, in the top 15.

From the Tour DuPont it was back to Minneapolis for three days, then off to Pittsburgh, West Virginia, New Jersey, and then Philadelphia for the USPRO Championships. Despite a somewhat promising Tour DuPont, none of my rides in these races were inspiring. By the time the CoreStates USPRO Championship in Philadelphia came along, I felt like I was simply punching a clock.

Nonetheless, we all lined up in Philadelphia with the goal of getting one American member of the Coors Light team into the stars-and-stripes jersey of the U.S. national champion, if not on the very top step of the podium (the race was open to riders from all countries, and the U.S. championship was awarded to the first American to cross the finish line, whether he won the race or not). An all-too-early breakaway dashed those chances, and despite being in that breakaway, my day ended early after a long chase robbed me of any remaining desire to ride by myself for an also-ran placing.

I called it a day and made my way back to the feed zone and team tents that were provided by the race organizers. Since the USPRO Championship was celebrating its tenth anniversary, the good people at the Coors Brewing Company had seen fit to make us some commemorative USPRO Championship 16-ounce Silver Bullets—a lot of them. Roberto Gaggioli, who had also pulled out of the race, showed up about the same time I did, so the two of us toasted the end of another USPRO Championship with a cold beer. It had been a hot day, and the first ones went down pretty quickly. We had a second and then a third. As I cracked my fifth or sixth commemorative Silver Bullet, a man with a clipboard entered the tent and told me I had been picked as a random for doping control.

I signed the papers, and he gave me directions to where the control was being held. I somewhat clumsily climbed back on my bike and headed over to pee in a cup. I rode my bike into the hotel lobby and spied one of the UCI officials sitting on a couch.

"It's right upstairs," he said. "You can't miss it. Follow the signs."

I leaned my bike against a giant potted plant and proceeded up the stairs to the single hotel room that was being used as the control room. The testing doctor was wearing a brightly colored polo shirt with the U.S. Olympic Committee logo emblazoned proudly on the chest. Two young girls were also present, his daughter and her friend. The list of UCI doping control protocol infractions was flying at my face almost faster than I could handle.

"Is this a USOC test?" I asked.

"Yes, we are using USOC testing procedures and a USOC approved lab" came the answer.

At that moment my ever-so-faint feeling of doping-control persecution shook hands with the five or six beers swimming around in my bloodstream and took control of the ship. I ranted on about how this race was sanctioned by the UCI and therefore didn't fall under USCF/USOC jurisdiction. With so many elements of the UCI testing protocol being broken, a rider could pee straight amphetamine and walk away without punishment, as if he'd gone to trial for murder when all the evidence had been illegally obtained and the arresting officers had failed to read him his Miranda rights.

After going through the process of peeing in the cup, I completed the rest of the USOC's procedures and then informed every other English-speaking member of our doping-control club that the control itself was worthless.

As luck would have it, one of the top three finishers had banned stimulants in his system, but since the control was illegal, he was only stripped of his placing and never received any prize money.

***

Back home in Minnesota, I was able to cherry-pick a few races here and there, but as in the two preceding years, I mostly rode mountain bike races and trained for the last major goal of the season, the Norwest Cup. The team was still on the road regularly, with small stage races and criteriums happening just about every weekend, but after being on the road and racing for close to an entire month, the little weekend trips didn't seem like enough to keep up my fitness.

As the summer wore on and September drew near, I was asked to do promotional appearances for the Norwest Cup. My teammate Chris Huber had won the race in 1993, so he came to town a few times for the same events or similar appearances. After the disaster of the previous year, I really wanted to have a good ride in this race, which was taking place just 2 miles from my front door. I knew I would have a job to do that would most likely keep me from any big result, but if I could help get one of my guys on the top of the box, things would be great.

I heard that José de Cauwer was going to be coming to the Norwest Cup, so I arranged to meet with him the day before the race for a cup of coffee. Though he'd spoken mostly English to me when I had been riding for him in Belgium, José spoke only Flemish to me in the restaurant in downtown Minneapolis. My own Flemish was only this side of nonexistent, but neither of us gave up. I knew I was only a shadow of my former self, but the meeting with this former mentor inspired me in a way that would otherwise have been possible only with copious amounts of illegal substances.

I rode my bike downtown on race day, knowing I would not have a chance of winning but that I would twist my own balls off in order to make sure the race was controlled and that my teammates were given every opportunity to win if they had the legs to do so.

I stayed in the top 10 to 20 riders all day long, but in the end the Coors Light Team came up a bit short. I even made an anemic attack for a bit of cash in the last kilometer of the race but ended up getting passed by almost everyone in my group 20 or so meters before the line.

Later that evening, after many of the racers had gone back to their hotel rooms, José and I enjoyed a couple of beers in the same bar where I had celebrated the end of my racing career the year before. I was in an entirely different mood now, thinking I had at least a few more years with Coors Light in front of me. José bragged to anyone who would hear him about my ability to control the day's race. His chest was as puffed out as any good father's could possibly be, but in the same breath he told me that he had known all along that this was the kind of life I needed to be living. It was, all at once, the greatest compliment and the greatest criticism I have ever received.

4

TEXAS BROOM WAGON

IN BLUE-COLLAR CYCLING'S TYPICAL ANTICLIMACTIC FASHION, the 1994 season was over, and I found myself in a position that was all too familiar: I had no new contract in hand. The Coors marketing folks decided a women's baseball team was a better use of their dollars than a cycling team. At that point Coors had been continuously involved in cycling for more years than almost any other company in the world. Seeing as how I was really the only one on the team who even drank the free beer that sponsorship afforded, the change might have been warranted. Len had been in negotiation with several different sponsors to fill in for Coors, and I knew I would have a spot if he landed something, but as other riders on our squad went elsewhere, the beer money seemed increasingly difficult to replace.

I had spent $1,500 of my recently paid-out prize money on a brand-new black-and-white laptop computer and was busy learning how to mess it up. E-mail was still a novelty in 1994, but the Coors team had been on the cutting edge; just about everyone on the team traveled with a computer, and I had been e-mailing my teammates via my Apple Newton, which was, of course, one of the biggest and least useful PDAs ever built. But since I kept screwing up my laptop, I was still using the Newton for e-mail. At about the same time all hope was lost for a new iteration of the Coors Light Cycling Team, I got an unexpected e-mail from my former Coors Light teammate Michael Engleman.

"Diamondback is looking for road riders to race mountain bikes," it read. "Call Keith."

I dialed the number right away and got Keith Ketterer, Diamondback's race team manager, on the phone.

"Hello, this is KK," said the voice in a tone that sounded eager to talk and completely behind schedule at the same time.

"Uh, hi, Keith," I started, temporarily derailed by his nickname. "This is Joe Parkin. I am a professional cyclist with Coors Light. Michael Engleman told me you are looking for road pros to start racing mountain bikes."

"That's not entirely true," he answered. "It's interesting that he would say that, but why don't you go ahead and tell me a bit about yourself?"

I proceeded to give him the short version of where I had been and what I had done, explaining that I had been anxious for a couple of years to give mountain bike racing on the national and international level a try. From a somewhat unsure start the conversation moved quickly through a preliminary interview to a second interview and fell just short of salary negotiations. I agreed to fax him my résumé posthaste, and he promised to get back to me within a day or two. Once again I was filled with hope for a new contract.

The courtship between Diamondback and me was probably the shortest in my cycling career and moved quickly to a salary offer and the delivery of a contract. Since I had resigned myself to working retail and donning a bright orange Scott/BiKyle jersey for select events, the $20,000 base salary from Diamondback sounded like big money—huge money. I scribbled my signature at the end of the 17-page contract and overnighted it to Diamondback headquarters in Camarillo, California, before any of us could change our minds. Two days later a most extravagant care package arrived, consisting of a titanium Diamondback Racing (DBR) road bike and a "welded carbon-fiber" DBR mountain bike—and these were just for training. I'd have separate bikes to race. There were also spare cables, spare chains, stems of various lengths, and a host of miscellaneous other goodies. Pro bike racers never, ever get over receiving the season's new bike, and this brought that feeling to an entirely new level. It was like Christmas in my basement.

Nearly a decade after signing my first professional contract, I was switching gears and going mountain bike racing full time. Making this change renewed my enthusiasm for bike racing in a way I had largely forgotten. I started looking forward to hard training the way most people look forward to a casual ride with friends. The popularity of cross-country mountain bike racing was still climbing toward its peak, and while the heart of cycling still beat hardest on narrow European roads, mountain bike racing seemed to be gaining ground by the acre. The young off-road discipline was booming with new technology. It was flashier and sexier than its road relative, and it seemed that much of the younger talent in cycling was headed toward the dirt rather than the staid road scene.

Most of the stars of the American road scene could come across like buttoned-down types from corporate boardrooms, but the personalities in mountain bike racing were extravagant and outrageous. Downhiller Greg Herbold wore strange neon ensembles and spoke with his own unique vocabulary, a mish-mash dialect pulled from the SoCal hot-rod scene, dirt bikes, skateboarding, and some nutty high-octane hipster part of his soul. Missy Giove, another downhiller, wore a nearly petrified dead piranha on a necklace, flaunted her tattoo and Mohawk, and happily discussed her love of girls over boys. Instead of canned, stoic answers presented in an uninspiring monotone, riders from all mountain biking disciplines used fantastic hand gestures and motorcycle sounds to describe, with great animation, very short sections of trail. Riders assumed nicknames such as *Earthquake Jake, HB, The Missile, Insane Wayne, Hibachi,* and *The Tomes*—nicknames that were more suited to matinee wrestling than traditional bike racing. The scene resembled the human-powered equivalent of pages stolen from a motocross magazine, with box vans, fifth-wheel trailers, and semis decorating the major race venues. And whereas road racing of that era boasted gradual equipment developments, the hardware in mountain biking was evolving and improving so rapidly that riders became vital in the testing and development process. Shimano, for one, had its legendary Skunk Works program to thrash and perfect its component designs, and the heroes of the sport could often be seen racing with prototype parts so new that they still bore the machine marks from the lab.

I'd raced some local mountain bike events, but I had only seen pictures of the bigger events in the United States and Europe. The crowds in the photos were huge, especially in Europe, where it seemed as though the entire continent had gone nuts over this new sport. After living as a deeply ingrained foreigner in Belgium and then continuing my road career as a citizen foreigner in the United States, I finally felt like I was coming home. It was as if I was finally a part of a true American contribution to cycling.

As with all endeavors that have ever interested me, going to the dirt side was not going to be a walk in the park. The preceding years had seen the world of cross-country mountain biking become inundated with ex−road racers like me who were not being welcomed with open arms by much of the off-road establishment. This was due in part to the fact that Americans were suddenly having a hard time finding the World Cup podium as more and more Europeans embraced the sport, but another factor was that many of us were seen as taking jobs from mountain bike racers who had "paid their dues."

I would have to learn, relearn, and refine a host of new skills, but first I needed to escape Minnesota to find some fitness. I called my friend Chris Robinson, the former road manager of 7-Eleven's junior program in Northern California, and asked if I could crash at his house for a few days so I could train on familiar roads—ones that weren't covered by snow and ice. Chris had apparently forgotten that "a few days" to a bike racer could mean almost anything, and I am quite certain that he wasn't thrilled with the thought of translating this to his wife after he learned that my stay was going to be three weeks. Despite that, I hung around and further rekindled the passion I had for two wheels on roads I knew almost well enough to ride blindfolded.

My first race of the season was in Lajitas, Texas, a sleepy little town on the Rio Grande that boasts a beer-drinking goat as its mayor. The race was part of a Texas state mountain bike series, so it drew all the local hopefuls as well as a decent amount of stars from the NORBA national series. Gunnar Shogren, Kendra Wenzel, and I would be representing DBR. Our teammates Dave Wiens and Susan DeMattei were opting out, and as this was not a race for the downhillers, Dave Cullinan and Jake Watson were not there either. For Kendra and me, this was to be our first test in the DBR colors, as she was also a transplant from the skinny-tire world. It was hardly the most prestigious event on the calendar, yet I was buzzing with nervous excitement; you'd have thought I was heading off to the first World Cup round or something. I was dying to test myself on unfamiliar terrain against unfamiliar riders.

Gunnar and I ventured out on a little ride the day before we raced to dust the cobwebs off our legs and out of our winter-soaked brains. The two of us bonded quickly, partially due to our similar hairstyles. In many ways Gunnar reminded me of my friend Gene Oberpriller; they were both bike riders to the very core. Both were also absolute legends in their own regions. Both bore the scars created from a lifetime of riding faster and harder than talent necessarily allows. We swapped the lead a few times on our short ride. While we both were definitely testing, neither of us was racing the other. We were moving through the scenery at a fast clip, though, and when Gunnar put a wheel wrong in a short little rocky section, I was close enough to stuff my front wheel into the back of his leg before the brakes could get me stopped.

With several miles of flat, twisty terrain before the climbing began, Lajitas's cross-county course was one that suited me well. After lining up for the race, I was pleased with my decent start, but the tempo was almost too much for my legs. I knew we weren't going all that fast, and I didn't have any reason to think anything was wrong with my bike, but I had the distinct impression that the brakes were rubbing—either that, or the bottom bracket was seizing up. Every racer knows this feeling; you know nothing is actually wrong, but the legs trick your mind into believing it's the bike's fault. In Europe they call it being "blocked," and when it happens to you there are usually only two possible outcomes: You'll either ride through it and the legs will miraculously begin to feel better than ever, or they'll simply continue to be blocked and your day will quickly become a complete disaster.

By the time we made it to the hills, my legs were coming around. I was able to do most of the big climb in the front group, losing only a few seconds. But it was going downhill that gave me grief. We were descending a long, narrow spine when I started to think about crashing. On the road I never thought about crashing while I was riding. I have awoken several times in the middle of the night in a complete, sweat-soaked panic after dreaming of flatting right at the apex of an outside turn of a long mountain descent, but the thought of crashing while actually riding down-hill had never before even entered my head. The spine we were descending was not particularly exposed, nor was it technical in any way—it was just fast. A small mistake would surely be pain-ful. As the crash-angst daymare was just about cleared from my brain, I misread a movement made by the rider in front of me. I hit a small g-out wrong—a deep rut that could swallow a bike—and my rear tire simply exploded. It was loud enough to make me duck, and I wondered if I needed to look for a bullet wound on my body. The sudden, catastrophic tire failure also managed to throw me off my line just enough for me to slam the rear wheel into a few too many rocks. The phantom brake-rubbing feeling I had had at the start was now a reality.

I rolled slowly down the rest of the descent before I stopped to see what repairs I could make. My race was finished, but I was still a long way from the finish line. I had no idea where I was and no idea how I was going to get back to town. The tire and tube were a complete write-off, so I took off the back wheel and removed the useless rubber. I stuffed the tube in one of my pockets and shoved the shredded tire up under the back of my jersey. It was my first day on the new job, so to speak, and I was not even going to finish.

The trouble with having to continue on a bare rear rim was that much of the rest of the Lajitas course was sandy, so I was getting nowhere fast and doing a pretty good job of getting in other people's way. In mountain bike racing it is not always easy to know when a faster rider is approaching, especially when the closing speed is high, based upon my limping speed. I continued wallowing along the narrow, shallow slot canyon, turning my head to look behind me every couple of seconds. One would naturally expect that after riding thousands of miles per year holding a straight line while turning to look backward over my shoulder, this little excursion should have been a cinch, but just before I turned to look forward again I plowed smack into the side of the little canyon. I climbed off my bike and started walking. Before too long there was a road crossing. A course worker told me the road would take me back to town, but that it would be close to 10 miles. Riding 10 miles with a bare rear rim on asphalt seemed like a much better plan than walking the however-many-miles-left-to-go of the racecourse, so I turned right and headed for home. It turned out to be the right decision because within a mile or two some kind race workers in a pickup rescued me. I suppose getting to the finish line in a broom wagon was a fitting start to my mountain bike career, but I was certainly hoping things would improve.

Kendra and I continued to campaign the Texas state series, the California state series, and any other regional event where the Diamondback sales reps thought a little factory race representation would be useful. It was a cool gig, really. We'd fly in on Thursday night; Friday morning we'd perhaps do a shop visit or two. We'd check out the course and then race on Saturday or Sunday.

Kendra seemed reluctant to ditch the familiar ways of road and track racing for the relative chaos of mountain bike racing. She was incredibly strong and had great potential as a mountain biker, but I think she wasn't having quite as much fun as I was.

Nevertheless, while we didn't always win, we were always on the podium, so everyone was happy.

In addition to the regional events, there was also the NORBA National Championship Series (NCS) to contend with. Diamondback's big stars, Dave Wiens and Susan DeMattei, were to focus primarily upon the UCI World Cup and NORBA National events.

Round one of the NORBA NCS was held in Spokane, Washington. The course, which had been moved and modified from its original plan, was a reasonably flat and fast one that consisted primarily of logging service roads. As a rookie on the mountain bike circuit, I started from the back. It was a completely nontechnical course, although large puddles of water scattered throughout hid bone-jarring, square-edged bumps and holes. The ground was soft enough to sap the energy from a rider's legs in no time. The race went by in a blur of mud-spattered confusion and inspired boredom. The only thing that kept me awake, I believe, was the rich smell of pine trees and the occasional splash of freezing water on my shins. I had thoroughly enjoyed the regional racing I had been doing, but this National was a different story. It seemed like a lot of hype with little excitement or reward. What I had anticipated to be a technically demanding circuit ended up being a mountain bike race on fire roads.

I'd largely eschewed my road bike for the mountain bike at this point. I was growing increasingly annoyed with people telling me how as a former roadie I might—perhaps—manage to ride well in races that were purely physical and required no technical mountain bike skills whatsoever. My thought was that if I were to train hard on my mountain bike, I would most likely be able to ride it with some semblance of skill even when my heart rate was nearing its 186-beats-per-minute max and my eyes were crossed.

When I started racing at higher altitudes, though, I began to wonder what I was doing in the sport. Although I was always able to produce a large amount of power and had a decent, if not respectable, VO$_2$max, my hematocrit level seldom reached even the low to mid-40s, meaning I would never be able to climb to even my own mediocre level in a race at altitude. It really didn't matter how I attacked my training or these high-altitude races; I was never going to do anything important in any of them.

Back at home I could enjoy totally dominating the local scene in both road and mountain bike events, but as a pro, that was of little comfort. I started thinking about a return to the road, even if it meant another yearlong sentence in a minivan, traveling the Eastern Seaboard in search of criteriums.

Nineteen ninety-five marked the last year in the Norwest Cup contract, and as the local pro, I was still counted upon to help with publicity even though I was now a mountain bike racer. I was also looking forward to getting back on the road after a half season on the dirt. I felt I always knew my place in the grand scheme of cycling, but it is still nice to be recognized as an expert in one's field versus being resented as the new guy—or worse, a "fucking roadie."

The Norwest Cup was to be held earlier in the year this time around, which pleased me because I could then concentrate on it as well as Chequamegon. Leading up to the event, I was interviewed by the print press and asked to talk about the race on most of the local radio and television talk shows. Cycling, with its marginal popularity, proved somewhat difficult for the evening and late-night news broadcasters to get their arms around, so I was most often asked to come in for the early-morning shows. This is all well and good, but dressing up in full cycling regalia for a show that starts earlier than 6 A.M. is often rather humiliating, especially when you're also asked to talk about bicycle safety and helmet use in the context of an actual bicycle race. Each time I stared at another female weatherperson's heavily powdered facial hair at 6:13 in the morning, answering inane questions about how to properly wear a bicycle helmet, I wondered how many NFL linebackers ever made it to the studio in time for such an interview.

I knew from the gun that I lacked both the legs and the desire to ride well in the Norwest Cup. Still, I suffered along, hoping to find some asphalt-based redemption to my otherwise horseshit mountain bike career. Try as I might, however, I was already a mountain bike racer and lacked the speed to give me any chance of a good ride in Minneapolis. I struggled with the pace from the giddyup, and the rare, oppressive heat and lack of a downtown breeze further hindered my attempt at a comeback.

Embarrassed, I climbed off my bike and abandoned what would turn out to be the last UCI-sanctioned road race of my career. I may have wanted to come *home*, but I was clearly no longer welcome in the colony.

Next on the NORBA docket was the National at Traverse City, Michigan. I was definitely looking forward to the event, if for no other reason than the fact that I would at least be suffering, and perhaps sucking, at sea level as opposed to 7,000 feet. Since all my relatives lived there, I always counted Michigan as my ancestral home. I wanted to put in a good ride to do my family proud, although my results in the previous NORBA Nationals suggested that anything better than a 50th place or a did not finish (DNF) would have been a bonus.

The Traverse City course was home to an infamous water jump and a host of other obstacles that offered options in how to attack them—options that also meant a slight time penalty. I'd heard morbid tales of the water jump and was anxious to see it. Upon arrival at the venue, Gunnar and I set out on a reconnaissance lap of the course. We rode up the little climbs and wove through the trees without incident; there really wasn't anything spectacularly exciting or technical about the course or its obstacles—except, perhaps, for its water jump. When we rolled up to it, I nearly instantly lost all motivation when I saw that a rider who had tried to clear the jump had come up short and crashed. I had built more jumps as a kid than I can remember, but now I was feeling too much like an old road racer. Seeing a 20-year-old lying on the ground, writhing and screaming in pain after having missed the landing and apparently broken bones in the process, was not terribly inspiring.

"Fuck it," I told Gunnar. "I'll just take the option."

In an attempt to give racers a way to get around the course's man-made obstacles, the course designers had built an alternative route, or "option," around each one. Though definitely safer and perhaps easier, the option detours also took longer—perhaps as much as 5 seconds.

"No, c'mon, ya big sissy," he countered. "We'll do it. You just follow me."

We rode back up to the point that marked the start of the descent toward the water jump, turned around, and started toward it. I marked Gunnar's speed precisely. All at once I was airborne and then back on the ground, without any broken bike parts or bones. It was as easy as that.

"Wow, that guy must really suck," I said, glancing again at the fallen rider. Gunnar just giggled.

After the gun I quickly found myself in the lead group of roughly 15 riders. Strangely, this was one of the easiest races in which I'd ever competed. It felt amazingly similar to any number of kermis races I'd ridden where I'd been part of a break that had gotten away at precisely the right moment with precisely the right people, resulting in a virtual shutdown of everyone else in the race. There seemed almost no reason to even pedal hard.

Nevertheless, we pushed on, and the attrition rate began to mount. As for me, I slowly lost most of my power and spark in the heat and humidity of the Michigan summertime, but I finished 10th anyway. Tenth was not a great result, but it was a tangible sign that I was starting—ever so slowly—to figure out this mountain bike thing. Just a week ago at the Norwest Cup I had been a man without a country, without a profession, and seemingly without purpose. Now I was finally feeling like a mountain biker.

5

PAYDIRT

WITH PLEASANT MEMORIES OF MY RECENT 10TH-PLACE FINISH AT the NORBA National Championship Series event in Traverse City fresh in my mind, I was hoping for a good ride in Helen, Georgia. Another dry, fast, sea-level race was exactly what I needed. The weather in this goofy little wannabe German town didn't want to cooperate, however, and after some soaking rain the course was a mess. I had made a habit of arriving at the NORBA venues early—earlier than my teammates in some cases—because with time to spare, I could put in enough laps to memorize the course and make sure everything on my bike was perfect, or at least as perfect as it could be. But for this race I got into Helen with just one day to sort out the course.

On Saturday I set out for some reconnaissance laps, and the budding good attitude I had about my career as a mountain bike racer shriveled up and died. The rain had stopped and the course was now drying just enough to stick every last bit of thick Georgia mud, every piece of dead grass, every pebble, and every cigarette butt to my tires. My bike felt as heavy as a loaded Boeing 747. Add to that the fact that I seemingly had forgotten how to ride my bike upon arrival in the Peach State, and the single sighting lap I was making turned into an internal battle while I struggled not to hurl my bike into the woods and call a cab. I generally liked hanging out in the team area, but when I finally made it back to the start/finish area I'd had enough and called it a day. The mechanics wanted to know if I needed anything special done to my bike.

"Fuck, for all I care you don't even need to wash it," I complained. "This sucks."

I headed back up the hill to the house I was sharing with Jake and Cully (Dave Cullinan). The house was hotter than hell. It seems that in an attempt to lower the temperature on the thermostat, Jake had broken the thing and no cool air was flowing at all. I suppose I had been just tired enough the night before to be able to sleep, but now the idea of staying in this sauna wasn't making me happy. I jumped in my rental van and headed to the house where Dave Wiens, Sue, Gunnar, and Kendra were staying, assuming their place would be nice and cool. I was shocked to find the temperature equally uncomfortable.

"Is the AC broken here also?" I asked.

"No," Dave answered.

"Well, let's get it going, eh?"

"No AC," said Dave. "We're getting acclimated."

"Serious?"

A pose that's as goofy as my haircut. I honestly loved that bike, though.

A sheet of hero cards from 1994, the last year of the Coors Light Cycling era. We were definitely the most cohesive squad in the United States.

I loved riding for Len
Pettyjohn, the Coors
Light team director.
He was a great leader
who always got the
most out of his riders.
(TOM MORAN)

I'd be hard-pressed to think of a better in-race tactician than Scott Moninger. (TOM MORAN)

I was never fond of the uniforms, but riding for the dominant U.S. team and getting free beer had definite advantages. (TOM MORAN)

The magazine spread below is from the August 1994 issue of *Winning*.

Studs In Their Duds
WHAT THE PROS WEAR

Thought and technology go into every piece of cycling clothing available to the pros — and to you, too.

by Tracy L. Seip

Technology is almost always subject to the trickle-down effect. High-tech theories, manufacturing techniques, and products are constantly being created and developed by governments and multi-million dollar corporations. Such technology is eventually adapted and made available, at relatively affordable prices, to the general public. This process holds true for most products on today's market, including cycling clothing.

The leading-edge cycling clothing worn by Tour de France winners and national and world champions is available to riders of all ages and abilities. On some cases exact team colors or logos are not available.) Cyclists can easily go up a top-quality jersey.

The new generation of cycling clothing features advanced fabrics like Aloft from Pearl Izumi, Aussie's Dry Ice Temperature Control, and Air-Pore by Ultima, which were specifically designed to wick moisture away from the skin quickly and efficiently. This wicking process keeps the rider relatively cool and dry, not sweaty and sticky. An added bonus is that these materials wash well — retaining their original color, shape and feel.

The overall fit and comfort of cycling clothing are two more

important considerations taken into account during the manufacturing process. Many jerseys feature raglan sleeves, long zippers and deep back pockets. Shorts are form-fitting, yet not constrictive. Chamois have become quite high-tech, too, and are now made with natural or synthetic leather or suede and anatomically positioned seams.

Winning examined clothing worn by four teams that competed in this year's Tour DuPont — Coors Light, Coldstrip, Saturn and Chevrolet/L.A. Sheriff. Prices for these top-of-the-line clothes are quite reasonable. The jerseys run from $52-70; while shorts cost $60-70. Socks retail for $6-10, gloves sell for $20-25.

Chevrolet/L.A. Sheriff
(as modeled by Bobby Julich)

+ Aussie Jersey — Made of Dry Ice Temperature Control material (wicks away moisture, but retains some moisture which reacts with the wind to allow for natural cooling; three pockets, five-inch zipper. Sizes small through extra-large. Suggested retail price: $62.
+ Aussie Shorts — 7.5-ounce nylon/lycra, triple-layer polyester moisture-wicking synthetic suede chamois; elasticized waist and leg grippers. Sizes small through extra-large. Suggested retail price: $62.
+ Aussie Socks — Made of CoolMax. Sizes small through large. Suggested retail price: $6.

Coors Light
(as modeled by Joe Parkin)

+ Pearl Izumi Aloft Jersey — Made of Aloft for quick wicking; 50 cm hidden front zipper (team jerseys feature a longer zipper); saddle cut shoulder; elastic cuffs and waist; triple back pockets. Sizes small through extra-large. Suggested retail price: $69.95.
+ Pearl Izumi Pro Short — Made of nylon and spandex; eight panels; Ultrasuede Chamois system. Sizes small through extra-large. Suggested retail price: $69.95.
+ Pearl Izumi Attack Sock — Lightweight cotton, nylon and elastic. Sizes small through large. Suggested retail price: $6.95.
+ Pearl Izumi Pro Glove — Amara palm with light padding; sublimated back; no closure. Sizes small through extra-extra-large. Suggested retail price: $19.95.

BOBBY JULICH
Teams: Chevrolet/L.A. Sheriff
Age: 22
Height: 6 ft.
Weight: 140 lbs.
A new addition to the Chevrolet/L.A. Sheriff squad, Bobby Julich is a rising star on the national pro circuit. The Colorado native is a great climber who can also hold his own against the clock. Julich placed second in the Hamilton Classic, seventh in the NJNB Classic and fifth in the Kmart Classic of West Virginia. At his 1994 Tour DuPont he powered to an impressive second place in the prologue and went on to finish seventh overall. A former national team member, Julich earned the Tour DuPont's Best Young Rider Award in 1991.

JOE PARKIN
Team: Coors Light
Age: 27
Height: 6 ft.
Weight: 152 lbs.
Joe Parkin's nine seasons of competition have included both American and European racing. In 1986 he headed to Europe to race for an amateur squad. After being denied a spot on the national team for the 1987 Tour of Belgium, Parkin turned pro. TVM offered him a spot on their team, but when the team's director sport quit, Parkin got out of his contract. After stints with Europ and Tulip and a 10th-place finish in the 1988 Tour of Belgium, Parkin returned home in 1991 and joined Scott/Elf/ule for the 1992-1993 seasons. Last winter Parkin talked with team director Len Pettyjohn and signed on with Coors Light. "Things are looking really good," says Parkin. "There are teams that are better than us in the PCF rankings, but we are really dominant here in the U.S." Parkin, who bears several tattoos, including one on his back of an Indian chief complete with headdress, recently finished 14th in the Cordivens Hamilton Classic.

I think Roy Knickman had more natural talent than I did,
but we both loved to control races. (TOM MORAN)

Keith Ketterer ran the DBR team with the precision of a fine timepiece. He was always a good cheerleader, too.
(MIKE MARTIN/ MORANPHOTO.NET)

Below, my DBR hero card.

In the thick mud of Helen, Georgia, on my way to a spot on the U.S. team for the 1995 World Championships. (TOM MORAN)

This *VeloNews* report from 1992 about Chequamegon was the first ink I got from mountain bike racing, but at that point I was still a full-time road racer.

LOCAL DIRT...

(Continued from page 32)
of 33 women this year, after 20 last year, and just two in 1990. "Organizer Grant Lamont took a tough lead, and we'll sure be back!" noted Sydor.
— Brent Mudry

CHEKANAUS CHALLENGE, Whistler, B.C. October 4.

Pro-expert men: 1. Bruce Spicer (Rocky Mountain), 63km in 2:33:45; 2. Don Bascombe (Brodie), at 0:06; 3. Mike Travlin (Kona-Mystal), at 12:08; 4. Scott Hall (Beldek), at 13:20; 5. Dale Douglas, at 15:24; 6. Eric Crowe, at 15:55; 7. Chris Biskop, (Wesbane), at 17:42; 8. Mike Edwards, at 18:20; 9. Greel Albert, at 19:46; 10. Aart van Kooy, at 20:42.

Pro-expert women: 1. Alison Sydor (Kahlua), 63km in 2:58:46; 2. Lesley Tomlinson (Kahlua), at 10:46; 3. Jill Smith (Specialized-Pedal), at 18:14; 4. Dawn Titus, at 18:34; 5. Marcia Wood (Brodie), at 22:46.

Parkin speeds to Chequamegon

victory Below-freezing, pre-race temperatures gave way to sunny skies and warm breezes, on the morning of the Chequamegon 40, in Hayward, Wisconsin. Gone were the torrential downpours and at times impassable, muddy conditions that had plagued the 40 in the past two years. For this 10th edition, on September 19, 1600 fat-tire fanatics lined up to take on the country's largest mountain-bike event.

After a two-mile, motor-paced roll-out — from downtown Hayward, to the famed Rosie's Field access to the American Birkebeiner ski trail — Parkin hit the dirt, accompanied by Dewey Dickey, riding for the Como Wheelers of St. Paul, Minnesota, and Erik Ringsrud, on the Minneapolis-based Flanders Brothers-Univega team.

Immediately, Parkin put the hammer down. "It was the quickest I have ever seen the lead group break away," remarked pace driver Mike Cooper. Indeed, the three breakaways left the field gasping, with Parkin — who has ridden professionally since 1987 (in Europe, on the Tulip team, and currently with the Scott BiKyle-Flyers) — pushing the pace with his 23-year-old riding partner, Ringsrud, a former champion of the 40.

Past Chequamegon 40s had led the leaders to believe that the pack would be right on their tail, but the pace was too high. "I really blew up trying to tack on to them," commented ex-pro Tom Schuler. Schuler, who repeated his fourth-place finish of last year, was only one of many favorites who missed the break.

Missing from the event entirely was Greg LeMond, the two-time champion of the 40. Persistent, late-season infections forced LeMond to pass up the race.

Even the 23-year-old Dickey admitted, "Early on, I was cramping up and doing all I could do to just hang in. There was a lot of one-upsmanship when Erik or Joe would take the lead. It was as if they were seeing who could out-pull the other."

It was Dickey, though, who had the other two worried, just as they crested the top of the Seeley Fire Tower climb. "Dewey really motored when we hit the Birke Trail, just after the big climb," Parkin said. But the

Parkin set a fiery pace to win Chequamegon.

chasing pair tacked back on.

It was the last few miles of single-track that determined the winner. "Joe pulled away with about a mile to go," recounted Dickey. Parkin came in with a time of 2:18:12, eight seconds ahead of Dickey, with Ringsrud a further 19 seconds in arrears.

In the women's race, Muffy Ritz pulled away from her rivals, about eight miles from

the finish, to win with a time of 2:56:15. Ritz, from Ketchum, Idaho, finished two minutes ahead of second-placed Karen Waeschle.

No stranger to the trails of the Chequamegon, Ritz is a two-time winner of the American Birkebeiner ski marathon — held each February, over the same terrain as the Chequamegon 40.

Ritz was well aware of her competition, based on her second-place finish last year. "Karen beat me by 20 minutes last year," said Ritz. In fact, Waeschle attacked from the start, and was soon out of sight. Behind her, eventual third-place finisher Cindy Bijold (Erik's Bike Shop) passed Ritz about 10 miles into the race ... and it wasn't until halfway that Ritz regained her second-place position.

"On the section before the Seeley Fire Tower climb," recalled Ritz. "I heard her breathing hard, and kind of snuck by her with a male rider between her and myself. After that, I never looked back."

With her victory in the 40, Ritz, a coach and teacher for the Sun Valley Ski Education Foundation, became the only person to win both the Chequamegon 40 and the American Birkebeiner ski marathon.
— Gary Crandall (Cable, WI)

1992 CHEQUAMEGON 40-MILE, Cable, WI. September 19.

Men: 1. Joe Parkin, 2:18:12; 2. Dickey Dewey, 2:18:20; 3. Erik Ringsrud, 2:18:31; 4. Tom Schuler, 2:24:34; 5. Weintz Bittner, 2:24:40; 6. Scott Hebel, 2:25:07; 7. Randy Bailey, 2:25:36; 8. Larry Sorenson, 2:25:58; 9. Jeff Bradley, 2:27:25; 10. Brent Prenzlow, 2:28:29.

Women: 1. Muffy Ritz, 2:56:15; 2. Karen Waeschle, 2:58:34; 3. Cindy Bijold; 4. Tricia Baker, 3:03:44; 5. Mamie Laser, 3:05:45; 6. Kelly Kunkel, 3:10:30; 7. Kathie Janecek, 3:12:23; 8. Joann Hanowski, 3:13:02; 9. Vickie Roberts, 3:13:04; 10. Jessica Innis, 3:15:10.

A wonderful person and great racer, Susan DeMattei (shown here at Mt. Snow, Vermont, in 1994) won Olympic bronze in '96, then stopped racing to start a family. (TOM MORAN)

Flanked by some of the legends of the sport on the podium in Helen, Georgia, with Tinker Juarez on my right and Johnny Tomac on my left. My big swig of champagne came back out through my nose.

(TOM MORAN)

Nautilus Nutritionals / BARRACUDA
Professional Mountain Bike Team

Jeff Bicknell   Lisa Sher   Matt O'Keefe
Joe Parkin   Mike Janelle

The face of pain and suffering on the way to my first NORBA National Championship Series top 10 finish in Traverse City, Michigan. (TOM MORAN)

My head is circled as part of a "Find the pro, win a prize" promotion on this Barracuda hero card from 1997.

Lisa Sher was a solid gravity racer and a good friend. (TOM MORAN)

If you're lucky, you get a handful of truly brilliant rides in your career, and one of my best was in the Minnesota state cyclocross championship in 1997. (CHRISTIAN KLEMPP)

The late Mike Janelle and me, waiting for our time trial starts at the 1997 Sea Otter Classic.

Gene Oberpriller on the right in the company of Mark McCormack and Jan Wiejak, going for it at the start of the 1995 U.S. Cyclocross Nationals. (TOM MORAN)

One of the great characters in American cycling, Rishi Grewal had flashes of absolute, pure genius on the bike and always had something funny to say.
(TOM MORAN)

"Serious." Dave wasn't joking. In fact, he almost seemed angry with me for asking. I knew that bike racers from Colorado were averse to air conditioning from my days on the Coors Light Team, but the hot, humid air was downright oppressive.

I hopped back in the rental and drove around, hoping to find a hotel with a vacancy. After a few unsuccessful attempts, I made my way to the last DBR team house, where all the staff was staying. Since each bed was taken, I had the option of sleeping on the couch in the delicious air conditioning or heading back to the heat and high humidity. I chose the couch.

We woke to wet, steady rain. I am sure many of the other racers were cursing the conditions, but I was honestly indifferent. I'd spent six years wearing a rain cape or at least packing one in my pocket. Rain is a part of so many days in Northern Europe that you either accept it or turn into a raving lunatic. On the road, rain changes the way you select gears, the way you corner, even the way races play out. I knew some Belgian riders who preferred a rainy race to anything else. I was never one of those types, but I was certainly not bothered by the race-day conditions in Helen either, and I was looking forward to getting this final NORBA race of the season in the books. Before the mechanics left the house, I asked them to put narrower tires on my race bike, front and rear. A narrow profile would dig into the mud, potentially giving me more traction.

When we got to the venue I checked my bike and adjusted the tire pressure down to just under 30 pounds per square inch. With the lower pressure, the tires would glance off wet roots, rocks, bumps, and bridges more slowly, giving me what I hoped would be an added split second of time to react and avoid a crash. For whatever reason, I was calmer than normal. Before the start of every other race this season I had been a near-insane bundle of nerves. I would find myself having to pee five, six, seven times before the start. I couldn't survive for more than 30 seconds without checking my watch. I would partially inflate a spare tube and wrestle it into my jersey pocket so that if I got a flat I could save a few seconds on the course putting the new tube into the tire. Then I'd pull the tube out of my pocket, check the pressure, and sometimes deflate it and refill it. I would absolutely dread the start and the race that ensued. But as I stood in the rain at this race, I was as calm as anyone could be who is about to inflict pain and suffering on his body for two and a half hours.

Thanks to a string of mediocre results in the series, I had collected enough points to give me a mediocre starting position, which is to say I was not stuck all the way at the back. In fact, I could actually see a sliver of the course ahead instead of an endless sea of other riders and bikes in front of me. I survived the national anthem, a terrible combination of a traditional version and Jimi Hendrix's Woodstock interpretation in which the segue from orchestral to rock-and-roll seemed to have been done by a tone-deaf DJ with only one turntable. We received our last-minute instructions and waited, in near silence, for the gun to go off.

I have spent most of my racing career being in the wrong place at the wrong time. It often seemed that if riders were going to tangle at an important moment during a race, somehow they would come to me. This race was not like that. The start was easy. I made an outside pass to gain about 20 positions less than 200 yards from the start line and continued easily rolling past guys I wouldn't even have seen if this had been a race at one of the mountain resorts. I quickly came up on Bob Roll and told him I was going to pass. The Blob wasn't having it, though, and instantly made himself wide, as if we were in the final laps of a Formula 1 race. I continued to try and he continued to keep me behind him until I successfully pulled off a slightly risky pass on a slippery corner. I kept at it, not really feeling as if I was going that hard. I didn't seem to be digging terribly deep.

About halfway through the first lap I caught Ned Overend and Rishi Grewal, who were riding in second and third positions. Tinker Juarez was already a minute clear. I was officially riding in a league with some of the heroes of the sport. I'd seen Tinker and Ned in magazine ads and posters since the days when mountain bike racing first started receiving media attention. They were the godfathers of cross-country mountain bike racing and were favorites for nearly every race. I'd known Rishi from both road and mountain bike racing and expected him to be a strong contender as well. We stayed in a cluster for the rest of the lap, but I felt that they should be going faster. We crossed the finish line together to end lap one. I was momentarily and pleasantly distracted from the effort when I heard the series announcer, Peter Graves, say, "Ned Overend, Rishi Grewal, and . . . umm . . . that's . . ." Shortly into the second lap I was all alone and in second place.

For almost the next 2 hours, I continued to ride alone. With the wet and nasty conditions, the woods were almost completely devoid of spectators. I was having a potentially career-saving, career-changing ride and enjoying the fun that goes along with sliding a bike in the mud, but I was terrified. It felt like I was rowing a boat across the ocean in the dark with no navigational equipment whatsoever. When I did see people I would exaggeratedly tap my right index finger on my left wrist, to where a watch would be, and call out, "Time, time." If you were to give that request in Belgium, even little kids would understand that you were asking for the time gap between you and whoever you were chasing and whoever was chasing you. Even if they couldn't yet tell time, the young Belgians would have been counting the seconds. The few folks on the course in Helen were not savvy to my request for information, but I was at least told the time of day once.

Halfway into the penultimate lap, I was caught and passed by Jan Wiejak, a Polish American cyclocross specialist from the Scott team. I made a halfhearted attempt to stay with him, but by that point it was more important for me to stick with my pace and not blow up. As the wheels became loosened from my wagon, my reaction time slowed and my bike-handling skills deteriorated. I was sitting too hard on my saddle and grimaced in fear every time I hit another rock or root and felt the impact resonate through the bike as the tire bottomed out. I didn't know where my chasers were, but I knew for sure that a pinch flat at this point would surely cost me 5 minutes or more—I was just too tired and sore to make a tire change any quicker than that. I started getting closer to crashing too, and I did throw it away once on a little bridge crossing. I needed the race to be over, the sooner the better.

When you ask that much of your body, there are milestones during the effort and at places on the course that feel almost as good as the finish line. In this race, as I hiked my bike up the steepest hill on the course and crested it for the very last time, I was able to breathe a sigh of relief because it really was all downhill from here, and I felt confident that I would finish on the podium. Crossing the finish line was more of a formality.

The shock started to set in just as I rolled over the line in 3rd place. I was ushered into a party tent where the press was waiting to interview the top finishers. It felt a bit like I was coming out of anesthesia. I could focus on people talking and understand what they were saying, but I could not talk. I was not so physically exhausted as to be incapacitated, but I had never expected to be part of any podium press conference on this day. Less than 24 hours before I had been ready to throw my bike in front of a train. I sat down on one of the cold folding chairs they had set up and drank some water. I was interviewed quickly, but the real story of the day was how dominant Tinker had been, winning by 7.5 minutes.

When most of the finishers had arrived, the top five of us made our way to the podium for the awards presentation. I climbed to the third spot on the box and looked out upon the faithful few who were waiting to applaud us. A single big bottle of champagne was opened and passed around. When it made its way to me, I hoisted it high in the air and took a giant suck from the bottle. The bubbles foamed in my mouth and throat, though, and I coughed champagne out of my nose. Peter Graves laughed, announcing to the crowd that I'd have to get used to handling my champagne in the future.

My 3rd-place finish at the NORBA final meant I was the second American. Each year at the final championship race of the season, the highest-finishing American who's not already in the world championship team selection, based upon points, is given a wild-card spot on the U.S. national team. In other words, I was going to get to represent the United States at the World Championships once again.

I quickly transformed my lackadaisical training program into something more appropriate for a rider who is headed for the Worlds. I upped the hours and intensity and took advantage of the various weeknight races Minneapolis had to offer. In Belgium, when I was trying to get ready for a big event, I would ride my bike to a race, compete, and then ride home again. Since the weeknight races in Minneapolis were significantly shorter than the stuff I had done in Belgium, I decided to put in three to four hours of training in the mornings as well.

The World Championships were to be held in Kirchzarten, Germany, in the heart of the Black Forest. For me, that was as good as a sea-level event. It also seemed to suggest a course that was free of extended climbs. I had absolutely no delusions of a podium finish in my head; I knew I would be starting at the back of the field, and since every rider who would be competing there was among the best his country had to offer, a high-placing finish would be tough. Still, my form was good, and with a little luck I thought I could at least be one of the top Americans.

The NORBA protocol dictated that all U.S. national team members arrive a week before the event. We DBR riders were on a different schedule, though, and had our own arrangements. Dave and Susan were going to Germany via the World Cup finals in Italy, and all of us would be in Germany for two weeks before the event, partly because KK thought it would be the best way to acclimate and partly because Dave and Sue had one more World Cup race a couple of weekends before the Worlds.

I arrived in the Frankfurt airport to discover that Dave, Susan, KK, and our soigneur John Cribari were stuck in Italy. A strike by airport workers was causing the cancellation of many flights, theirs being one of them.

I quickly called my pal John Podesta, who worked for Levi Strauss and was living near Frankfurt. After a little scolding for not giving him advance notice of my visit, John agreed to pick me up and put me up for the night.

Once everyone else arrived we loaded up a VW van and another rental car and made our way to the Black Forest. The U.S. national team had its own hotel, but we stayed in a small resort condo about 30 km away from the race venue in Kirchzarten. In perfect old-school European form, the resort's owner was an almost stereotypically boisterous, round German man, who, like most of the Belgians who frequented Albert and Rita's café in Ursel, was quite drunk by early evening and pontificated about nearly any subject that came up in conversation, whether he was a part of that conversation or not.

The Black Forest weather was rainy and cold, but we continued to train in the wet in the few days that remained between us and the World Championships. We hopped onto the official Worlds course for training as soon as we were allowed to, hoping to learn it well enough to be able to ride by Braille should we need to do so. Absolutely nothing on the 20-something-minute-long lap was interesting or memorable. In fact, I have ridden parking-lot road criteriums that practically equaled the level of difficulty that this particular mountain bike course provided.

As the days closed in on the big event, we moved our base camp from our condo in the trees to a proper hotel just a few kilometers from the course. I have never been a fan of condos anyway, so the move into a standard hotel room was a relief. When I raced on the road in Europe, teams never stayed in condos or any sort of host housing, so I had a hard time associating racing with sharing a house with a bunch of similarly obsessive bike racers. I much preferred the nearly prison-like feel of a Spartan hotel that didn't even pretend to make me feel at home.

My brother Jay, who was stationed in Germany with the U.S. Army, was able to come and see me now as well, which helped settle me down before one of the biggest races of my life. Since he had a little time off and I had an extra bed in the room, Jay was able to stay with me until after the race.

Two days before the cross-country World Championships, I bumped into the guys from Troy Lee Designs, who handed over a helmet smelling of fresh paint. Troy Lee's remarkable helmet designs were the high standard that every other customizer aspired to, and this helmet had been painted expressly for me and then signed by Troy himself. Just days after being awarded the Worlds spot based upon my performance in Georgia, I had called the company and asked if I could have a special helmet done for the Worlds. I requested that they retain some of the helmet's stock graphic design, but I wanted to add a waving American flag that began at the tip of the visor and extended all the way to the back. I had dreamed for years of having Troy Lee paint a helmet for me; I had always been a fan of motocross and the helmets he painted for the greats of that sport, so receiving my own custom helmet for this event was a proud moment. I felt almost as if I had finally arrived.

I was called to the start line in position number 132. Behind me was only one other row, but I had known from my wild-card status that it would go this way, and I was thankful and happy to be able to pull on the stars and stripes one more time. Unlike the beautiful USPRO colors that I had worn for the road and cyclocross World Championships, the national team mountain bike jerseys were hideous. Gone were the proud, patriotic stars and stripes, replaced by a sort of fusion jazz mix of red-and-blue vomit on an ill-fitting white polyester-nylon blend. It was, no doubt, conceived by the same deficient brain trust that deemed a medley of the traditional national anthem and Hendrix's version appropriate for the start of most NORBA Nationals. Nevertheless, I had been awarded a great honor and privilege in my opportunity to represent the United States again, so I kept my mouth shut and endeavored to do my absolute best.

The gun went off, and I watched for a few seconds as the riders in the many rows in front of me set off. After what seemed like 20 seconds or more, my row finally started rolling forward. The first kilometer was stop-and-go as nervous riders from all over the world pedaled too hard, closed in too tight on the riders in front, grabbed handfuls of brake, and then pedaled again. The first little climb, which most second graders could have ridden in their sleep, became a quagmire of chaos and mayhem, complete with punches, screaming, and fallen and trampled riders. It was clear that we would be walking for quite some time. In fact, I do not remember remounting my bike until just before the 4-kilometer marker, meaning that roughly 2 kilometers of the event had been a footrace. For my group, at least, this was becoming more of an extreme-walking world championship. Without ever getting my heart rate into anything close to race mode during the first lap, I lost 8 minutes to the race leader and eventual winner, Bart Brentjens.

As the race wore on, I felt better and stronger. I was improving at the same time that other riders were starting to fade, crash, or flat, opening up the course. Knowing I would not be racing for a win, a medal, or even a top-10 placing was boosting my confidence. I rode my own race, steadily picking people off on each section of the course.

World Championships are unique in that they present the opportunity for season-long rivals to set aside their differences and work together for their national teams. I was passing my own U.S. teammates as I rode, yet I was not happy to be beating them. Similarly, the Worlds were also breaking down some of the barriers between the various mountain bike disciplines, and I noticed members of the downhill team—normally indifferent to the cross-country scene, if not haughtily amused by it—cheering me on.

With a lap and a half to go, I had made my way up through the field into the 20s and was the third-best-placed American on the course. But that was also where the wheels started to come off the wagon. As had happened to me before, the easiest of obstacles—a root, a small rock, a low-hanging tree branch—became too hard to negotiate. Legs that had been more than willing to do whatever I asked of them were now going on strike. The cheers from the hordes of half-crazed bike racing fans that had spurred me on to victory just a lap or two before now sounded like muffled, unintelligible heckling. Once again the 2-hour mark was the beginning of the end for me, and one by one all of those riders I had passed now passed me back.

I finished the World Championships disappointed but not dejected. Starting where I had, I would have needed to ride faster than Brentjens just to come up with a decent finish—and even that result wasn't going to be much to write home about. I had prepared well and done the best I could, going all in on a long shot. I lost in a huge way, yet I was not ashamed for trying.

6

CYCLOCROSSED

AFTER THE 1995 MOUNTAIN BIKE SEASON WAS OVER, OUR DBR team manager, KK, sent Gunnar Shogren and me to New England to race cyclocross in preparation for the United States National Cyclocross Championships. It was a strange and wonderful return to cyclocross racing as well as a fantastic break from reality in many ways—two bike racers, lots of bikes, an expense account, and an empty house. Our focus was on improving our cyclocross skills and fitness, which was exactly what we did when we weren't hanging around the house. The little TV that came with the rental seemed to air nothing other than reruns of Matlock. Watching the aging former sheriff of Mayberry, North Carolina, solve crime made us wish the TV broadcast only in black and white and played nothing but old sitcoms. It is amazing how low a bike racer's tastes will sink when he is sequestered in a strange town.

The New England cyclocross scene was strong, if a bit inbred. The McCormack brothers—Frank and Mark—dominated each race, using a combination of solid cyclocross skills and some good old-fashioned road racing tactics to upset the balance of competition. Frank and Mark were so evenly matched in their strengths and bike-handling skills that I might easily have mistaken them for fraternal twins had I not known better. I would have been hard-pressed to pick the better of the two in any aspect of race craft, though Frank went uphill a bit better than his younger brother.

With two such equally matched opponents coming from the same family, the racing, while fast, was a bit boring from my standpoint as a competitor. Many races boiled down to a painfully frequently repeated finale: One of the brothers would attack, and I would chase, only to be counterattacked by the other brother as soon as I caught the original attacker. Chasing was a nearly fruitless endeavor on my part; I was not physically stronger than the brothers, and I definitely trailed them in cyclocross skills. As each race wound down toward the finish, I would do my best to hang on, and one of them would ride away. Now in the catbird seat, the brother not fortunate enough to draw the high card for the win would wait and attack me at the finish to take second.

Even though I felt relegated to reenacting a prime-time television script over and over, the experience provided me with a morale boost and a flashback to the days I had spent racing cyclocross, not only in Santa Cruz, California, with local and national legends, but also in the parks and fields of Northern Europe. It was a good feeling, and as the nationals approached I became more and more motivated to come up with a good result.

The 3.5 km championship course was laid out around the athletic fields of Leicester High School near Worcester, Massachusetts, and as soon as I saw it I knew I had a chance. Unlike the feeling of dread that had set in when I had first reconnoitered the NORBA National course in Helen, Georgia, earlier in the year, I immediately saw visions of climbing to the top spot on the podium in Massachusetts. The mountain bike course in Georgia had been thick with wet, dead grass and mud, but this cyclocross circuit was fast and wide, presenting opportunities for the wheel-to-wheel racing that I craved. The ground was hard, flat, and dry. Had there been bookmakers there, Frank and Mark would still have been the odds-on favorites, but I rated my own odds high against the other riders who would factor into the mix.

In bike racing, however, it seems that for every little glint of hope there's at least an equal amount of bullshit from the organizations that govern it. In every other country in the cycling world, pros would have been given a separate championship; in America, we were treated as the entitled minority. The "senior men" race in Massachusetts combined the field into a pro-am mix, and on the day of the race I knew we pros would be treated like lepers at a petting zoo.

In Europe the greats of the sport of cyclocross not only used their power and cyclocross skills to help them find the finish before the competition but also capitalized on the rules—or the lack thereof. I knew the start was going to be the biggest hurdle on the day because the powers that be would in no way respect the fact that bike racing is not a democratic election. Rather than having call-ups for the pros, in Leicester there would be a cattle call for all. I knew I would be fighting for my spot on the starting line, something I'd never done well. Perhaps it was my cold-climate roots, or perhaps just the fact that I never liked to dance, but the passive-aggressive, semi-intimate wrangling for a start position at the front that preceded each mountain bike race seemed like a waste of time to me. *You want to push me? Okay, I'll go ahead and punch you.* Since most race officials outside Minnesota have never seen a hockey game, I chose to grimace and hope I could make some worthwhile passes once the actual racing began.

Gunnar and I had prepared well for the race, putting in our training time, getting our bikes ready, setting up our pit plan for bike exchanges on each lap, and planning our race strategy. There was only one thing I had overlooked: the weather. The Leicester course was so tantalizing that I failed to imagine racing in anything but the pristine conditions we had seen. But race day greeted us with driving snow and bitter cold and deteriorated steadily as the clocked ticked down. The course was buried in a thick coating of snow and ice. I was almost instantly deflated. Riding in imperfect conditions was nothing new, of course, but I also knew that these conditions would negate any leg and lung strength advantages I had. The slippery conditions would make it a race in which not making any bike-handling bobbles would be the most important goal because stomping on the pedals most likely wouldn't result in an increase in forward momentum. I felt as out of place as a hippo in a pink tutu. Nevertheless, I found the starting line and did my best to avoid shivering to death or punching anyone in the mouth as I waited for the starter's pistol to fire. After some last-minute instructions, we were finally released onto the icy course, and the hell began.

The plan for Gunnar and me was to switch bikes when we reached the number-one pit on the first lap. Cyclocrossers in Europe had been pushing the rules of racing to their limit for years, and I intended to follow the tradition, perhaps gaining a few spots in the process. Entering the pits, I handed off my bike and then, using the rulebook vagaries to my advantage, squeezed through the other riders on my way to the end of the pit, where I grabbed one of my spare bikes. It was a move that would have made G. Gordon Liddy proud, and it moved us both into the top 15.

But the perverse grin that formed on my face halfway through the first lap quickly became a frustrated grimace. I desperately wanted to go harder. I wanted to stand up on the pedals and catch the guys in front of me. If the snow and ice had not come, I could have put in a 20-to-30-second effort and been racing for the win. But each time I made a push toward the front, the rear tire spun and I slid sideways, or fell. Catching a rider just 10 feet in front of me seemed to take an eternity. I felt helpless. Part of me wanted to get off my bike and throw the thing at the ground or some innocent spectator, and part of me wanted to soldier on. I opted for soldiering on.

Despite my deep desire to channel Swiss cyclocross star Thomas Frischknecht so that I could float gracefully over the snow as he does, I was wasting precious energy in my attempt to find the front of the race and eventually lost a place or two. With just a couple of laps to go, my teammate Gunnar caught and passed me. Ultimately we crossed the finish line in 7th and 8th place, respectively. I didn't care who won or where any of my friends had finished. All I knew was that the race was over and I could probably walk to the car with no worries of falling.

My bones were barely thawed by the time the news hit of the DBR team's relegation to the last two places. Complaints that Gunnar and I had cheated combined with the open eyes of pit officials didn't sit right with the race jury, so we were moved to the very bottom of the score sheet. For me, 8th place wasn't all that different from last. I knew I would have been in contention for the win had the conditions stayed dry, and the sting of that thought outweighed any punishment the officials could hand down. But KK and the people at Diamondback saw it differently, and rightly so, since a large portion of the budget had been spent on putting the two of us on the circuit. Without those two top-10 finishes, it would be hard to justify trying again.

Gunnar and I were tasked with arguing our case, both with the powers that be in Colorado Springs, where USA Cycling is headquartered, and with the press. I argued that no one at the race itself had been able to state a clear rule. For the first time in my cycling career, I read the official rule book. Try as I might, I was unable to find any sort of clarification as to how many steps could be taken without having contact with the bike. I found nothing to suggest that I wasn't allowed to pass another rider while inside the confines of a pit. I pored over video of the race and noticed that many other riders were running up to 10 steps without their bikes in hand. In fact, I counted 7 steps taken by the winner and defending champion, Jan Wiejack, before his mechanic handed him a clean bike. I wrote letters and made phone calls until I was thoroughly bored with the rules of cyclocross, with journalists, and especially with race officials. Alan Dershowitz may have approved of the loophole I found, but I had absolutely no desire to enroll in law school.

Perhaps it was that the discipline of cyclocross was a mere blip on the radar of American cycling, but a loophole existed, and we ran straight through it. I thought of the countless cars I'd held on to in my years of pro racing, the water-bottle hand-slings, the stories of doping controls that had been cheated. I remembered the times I'd shown up at a race for no other purpose than to sign in so my boss could collect the start money. Win or lose, I knew José de Cauwer would have smiled proudly at our attempt to exploit the rules to our advantage. Luckily for Gunnar and me, the cycling gods blessed us with a reversal of the National Cyclocross Championships jury's decision, and we were given back our placings.

7

OLYMPIC DREAMS

FRESH OFF A SOMEWHAT SUCCESSFUL SEASON, I ATTACKED MY preseason preparation for 1996 with a vengeance. Cross-country mountain biking was going to be an Olympic sport for the first time, and I was not completely out of the hunt for the last of the two spots. Most people weren't even willing to give me long-shot odds, calling my chances only a mathematical possibility. I didn't care what anyone else thought—I had a chance to go to the Olympics and to simply shrug off such a thing would have been inexcusable.

After the U.S. Cyclocross Nationals in December, I went back to Minnesota to cross-country ski and inline speed skate. I was still trying to ride my bike, but the weather was getting too cold for me. During my first off-season in the Land of 10,000 Lakes, I hadn't been able to keep my feet and hands warm while riding in temperatures below 20 degrees or so. I could cross-country ski in just about any temperature, though, and I also skated indoors, in the corridors of the Metrodome. I was starting to feel as I had when José de Cauwer had helped me figure out what kind of racer I was on the road. I had big motivation.

In January KK called to say that I had an opportunity to go to the Olympic Mountain Bike Camp in February. The camp would be held at the Olympic Training Center (OTC) near San Diego and would last almost three weeks. The last time I had been at an Olympic Training Center was for a developmental field hockey camp when I was 12. There was no way I was going to stay in the Minnesota deep freeze when presented with a chance like this.

As it turned out, the camp was slightly different than I originally envisioned. We were quartered at a hotel in Alpine, California, not at the OTC. The reason I was invited to attend was not because I was the number-six rider in Olympic selection points but rather because four of the five riders who were higher up the ladder didn't want to go. Most of the guys in attendance were part of the under-23 (U23) road team and were being coached by Roy Knickman. It almost felt like I was under 23 again because the future was looking brighter than ever.

I hauled both my mountain bike and my road bike out with me in a giant double-wide bike bag. We were mostly going to be training on road bikes, but since I was a mountain biker, leaving the other bike at home would have been like going to a job site without tools. On the first day of riding, the three mountain bike guys set out with the U23 guys and coaches Chris Carmichael and Roy Knickman. The plan was to ride out on a short loop so that everyone could warm up and then do some lactate threshold intervals. I was 29 years old and had raced all over Europe with some of the biggest legends of the sport, but I had never even heard of a lactate threshold (LT) interval until this camp. Before this I had adhered to the old European training mentality where you lay down a base of at least 2,000 kilometers before ever lifting the tempo to where you can't talk easily. Even after that you'd probably not ride too hard unless you were doing a team training ride. To find true fitness or "form" you had to race, period.

When we got to the bottom of the climb we'd be using for our LTs, I stopped for a minute to discuss a strategy for the day with Chris. He offered up a couple of ideas, and I set out, riding up the hill, keeping one eye fixed on the road ahead and the other on my heart rate monitor. The last time I had done any kind of physical testing had been in Belgium in 1991, so Chris and I took the results from then and subtracted a few more beats than normal to find the heart rate I would use as a target for the intervals. I would be riding uphill for 15 minutes at 170−172 beats per minute and then recovering by riding downhill for 10 minutes. Then I'd repeat the process. Sitting in the sun with a beer would obviously have been more pleasurable than purposely torturing myself, but as far as intervals go, these were pretty enjoyable. The effort was something I was intimately familiar with, having spent almost the entire 1991 Tour de Suisse riding at the front of the peloton, just a few beats away from being anaerobic.

My legs hadn't seen the sun since before the Mountain Bike World Championships the year before, and even though I'd ridden with bare legs in that race, I hadn't picked up much color. Now my legs were white. Snow white. *Minnesota* white. On my second or third trip up the hill, my old Coors Light teammate

Michael Engleman rolled up next to me. Engleman was even further from under 23 than I, but he was also hanging out in Alpine, also with big Olympic goals.

"Jesus, Joe, turn those things off," he pleaded.

"What?" I had no idea what he was talking about.

"Your legs are so white they're blinding me."

I finished my ride for the day and headed back to the hotel. There were only three of us at the camp so far, and it was looking doubtful that we would have any more male mountain biker company. I already knew Marc Gullickson pretty well. He had originally been a cross-country skier, but then he'd gotten interested in cycling to keep up his fitness and had gotten hooked. He'd raced on the road in France as an amateur and picked up mountain biking when he got back to the States. Marc is one of the friendliest bike racers you could ever hope to meet. I will never forget the congratulatory handshake and kind words he gave me when I made the U.S. national team for the World Championships. As it turned out, we finished a couple minutes apart at Kirchzarten, when Brentjens took everyone to school. We would never really be riding together at this camp, since it was designed around individual training programs and not big group rides, but it was still nice to have cool people around.

I would be rooming with John Weisenrider. John had no mathematical possibility whatsoever of making the Olympic team, but like me he had been invited to the camp when other riders had opted out. John and I weren't exactly the odd couple, but we also weren't much alike. He liked to spend his downtime in the room meditating, whereas I was busy fooling around with a new laptop computer I'd just bought and watching TV when he was not there. He also was a big fan of garlic—lots of it, which made our room smell like a roadside stand in Gilroy, California.

The days wore on and I started seeing some serious gains with this "new" form of training. I asked more questions and gleaned more knowledge from the top-level USCF coaching staff on hand. Carmichael was a big fan of "active recovery" techniques too, and I watched each day as the young road guys spent time aboard the super-skinny Kreitler Hot Dog rollers. The Hot Dog drums were only 10 inches wide, as opposed to 15 inches on the standard rollers, so there wasn't much margin for error. The idea behind the Hot Dogs was to make you a smoother rider because if you wove around you'd drop a wheel off the edge and crash. I'd been riding rollers since I was 16 years old, meaning since a lot of the other campers had been in grade school. I'd never stayed on rollers for more than an hour at a time while living in Belgium, but I had set a personal record of 8 hours in one day after moving to Minnesota. While in Belgium I had watched my friend, teammate, and former world professional pursuit champion, Colin Sturgess, make artwork out of riding rollers. He could ride them, jump off, and then jump back on again, and the rollers would never stop spinning. I could not perform roller ballet like Colin, but I could certainly ride the hell out of the stupid torture device, and one rare rainy day at camp I took the opportunity to show the young shredders how it was done in the old country.

I was dressed in the full '95 DBR regalia and climbed up on the Hot Dogs. I started riding along, or, as we liked to call it at the time, "doing birth control." As I rode I started sweating, and pretty soon I felt like I needed to shed a layer. Mountain bikers simply did not ride rollers in those days, so I was already a bit of a freak show, attracting the nonchalant gaze of a few of the young guys. There are only a few things I can (or could) do really well, and I am not humble enough to say I couldn't ride the rollers with some definite skill. So when I knew enough people were watching, I decided to take my hands off the bars and take off my jersey, all the while riding the skinny rollers. The young dudes didn't know how to react, and I received everything from blank stares to verbal expressions of disbelief. These were the best young bike riders America had to offer at the time, so each was cocky in his own way. And even though most of these young riders probably believed their road bike skills to be superior to mine, my roller striptease proved that I wasn't simply some brainless character from a Mountain Dew commercial.

As the camp continued, I was able to gather more and more information about training. To have any chance of making the Olympic team, we would need to match my training to the demands of the course that had been designed for the '96 games.

With decent fitness in my legs, I was looking forward to the season openers: the Specialized Cactus Cup in Scottsdale, Arizona, followed by the Sea Otter Classic at Laguna Seca Raceway in Monterey, California. Our bikes were quite different than they had been in '95. Instead of being decked out with a complete Shimano XTR component group—which, though expensive, yielded flawless race performance—our new bikes came with a bunch of parts from various manufacturers. The parts were fine, but they weren't necessarily designed to work together.

Once I got used to the new setup, I was okay with everything on my bikes except the tires. They definitely didn't like me. I had been getting too many flats while training, and in the opening cross-country race of the new season I flatted both front and rear. It was frustrating, but like everyone I knew except Lance Armstrong, who in his entire career has probably had fewer flat tires than I have gotten in one race, I had flatted before, and I supposed those two flats might be nothing more than an isolated incident.

I went to the Sea Otter in search of better luck keeping air in my tires. Although I hadn't set the world on fire the year before, I knew my fitness would be pretty good compared to that of most other riders there, not to mention that the thick ocean air was nice to breathe—a lot better than the thin vapor that would be coming my way soon enough once the NORBA circuit hit the mountain venues.

We were staying in downtown Monterey at a Travelodge or something similarly anonymous. It was a motel in dire need of immediate attention to the building's structure; the rooms could have used a cleaning too. Shabby quarters are common when you're traveling around playing bike racer, and I was used to them, but insult was added to injury when jackhammers, cranes, and dump trucks started to sound sometime before dawn.

We'd received most of our team clothing before the Sea Otter, but a few pieces were still supposed to trickle in. Oddly, the majority of the items we'd gotten were skinsuits. Skinsuits are just the ticket for time trials, nighttime criteriums, and cyclocross, but we were up to our necks in the things—too many, in fact, for most of the racing that we would be doing. When I found out that we were expected to race in skinsuits for cross-country races as well, I lost my cool. With a pair of scissors borrowed from the front desk, I started trimming my skinsuits into bib shorts. Of course the combination of my deplorable scissor skills and an already bad skinsuit design meant that my new bib shorts didn't fit very well. Luckily I managed to spare a few of the skinsuits from the blade because KK was none too happy with my behavior and had nothing for me to use as backup. My roommate, the always jovial Gunnar, belly-laughed himself silly.

The Sea Otter consisted of three stages: a time trial, a dirt criterium, and a two-lap cross-country. I had been doing so many intervals that I felt like a time trial would be no big deal, and in fact it went pretty well. When the launch signal was given, I rolled off the ramp and aimed my bike up the gradual climb between the track's turns 5 and 6. I felt like I was getting on top of the gear pretty quickly, which felt really good. Once I was off the track and into the dirt, the good feeling continued. Even though this was a time trial, in which pain and suffering abound and you're often tricked into thinking you're going either a lot slower or a lot faster than reality, I knew I was having a good ride. On the course's one steep and winding climb, I kept a relatively big gear turning over and even started to get the dizzy, almost blackout-like feeling in my head and in front of my eyes that was a signal that I was doing everything right. Once on top of the hill I was able to transition into a bigger gear with absolutely no hesitation—another good sign. For me, an obstacle like this hill in a time trial could easily have been the thing that caused my legs and body to seize up, wasting every previous gain I had made on the time trial course. Getting over the top without any signs of my motor sputtering meant the rest of this short stage was going to be okay.

Once I was able to see the track, I kicked it down once again and made my final push to the finish. I crossed the line gasping for air but recovered quickly. Our soigneur Alexa handed me something to drink and a long-sleeved jersey to keep me from cooling off too quickly. I had not set the quickest time but was well within the top 10—as was my new teammate, Cadel Evans.

Cadel was a great addition to the DBR squad but also a bit of a problem for me. The young Australian prodigy was definitely poised to be one of the best mountain bike racers of his generation. He was also a genuinely nice guy whom you couldn't help but like. But with all the attention he was getting, I felt like my shot at an Olympic berth was being neglected. The problem was compounded by the great results Susan DeMattei was getting. Cadel was a virtual shoo-in for the Australian team, and Susan's own Olympic spot was pretty much hers to lose. The lion's share of the team's attention and support was being aimed directly at the two of them, and rightly so; DBR was well positioned to send at least these two riders to the Olympics. But I'd been doing the math, and I knew I had a real chance of getting that last spot— something neither KK nor Bryan Seti, from Diamondback's marketing department, seemed to care about. With KK it was quite straightforward, and I could understand his perspective—he needed to protect his assets—so while I wasn't pleased, I dealt with it. Seti, on the other hand, seemed to want the rest of us to be cheerleaders, and though I had learned to reluctantly tolerate him the year before, in this new season I was already daydreaming about bashing in his skull with a floor pump.

When we lined up for the dirt criterium, I was called to the front row based on my good ride in the time trial. Even with a good start spot, I was apprehensive about the race; I wasn't sure

I would even begin to get my legs before it was over. Short races always seem to go one of two ways: Either you feel great and are racing for the win, or you're fighting with your bike and praying for the end of the world. Luckily, in this case I was blessed with the former. As soon as the gun went off I felt great. I never drifted outside the top 10 throughout the course of the 20-something-minute event. All of the heavy hitters of the day were there, but this race was not like a normal mountain bike race—it was a true wheel-to-wheel race, with attacks and counterattacks just like on the road. Part of me wanted it to go on for hours even though it hurt like hell. Having the presence of mind to watch my fellow competitors as closely as I was able and the legs to do just about whatever I wanted to do was always a truly incredible feeling. For some unknown reason, though, I began to think I was enjoying the experience just a little too much, and it interfered with my job. I knew I had the legs to do something big, but I had made up my mind to make sure I was in the top five instead of going all out. I never attacked, and I left myself at the mercy of my competitors' attacks. I got my top-five placing but should have won instead.

I was always a nervous mountain bike racer. My high heart rate at the starting line, my shaking hands, and my uncontrollable desire to pee dozens of times before the start of any mountain bike race were in no way enjoyable. But every so often I was able to approach a race with absolute abandon. I could smile and laugh. I didn't feel like peeing. The world was in complete order. I found this state on the morning of the '96 Sea Otter cross-country and thoroughly enjoyed it because I knew I was poised for a decent race. As on the day before, I was called to the front row based on my overall classification. This in itself was a huge bonus. Everyone who has ever raced a mountain bike knows that starting from the front makes getting to the first single-track section of the course much easier, whereas getting to the front of a mountain bike race if you have to start at or near the back—even for a race that starts on a wide asphalt road—is *extremely* difficult.

When we got the start command, I didn't disappoint myself. I stayed in the top 5 to 10 riders on the short, steep climbs and the descents that followed them. Perhaps it was the fact that I was actually riding at the front this year instead of halfway back in the group, but it felt like everyone was riding harder, as if everyone was gearing up for the first-ever Olympic mountain bike race. Cadel and I were riding close to each other until he mis-shifted and had to get off his bike to put his chain back on.

When we made it to the little climb that had been my moment of truth in the time trial, there was another bump-up in the tempo. I watched as several riders around me began to struggle to maintain the pace. I was still feeling good enough to hang on and quickly found myself in an elite group that included Tinker Juarez, John Tomac, and Rune Høydahl, the super-strong Norwegian who had won five World Cups in a row the previous year. The fact that I had made it into this early selection told me I was on the right track with my training and that the possibility of a podium place was well within my reach.

"Fast" is a relative term, but I honestly believe this was the fastest I ever rode in a mountain bike race. We were hauling ass. I had pulled myself up on the tip of the saddle, and my nose was just inches from the stem. The heart rate monitor I was using as a governor was useless at this point because I couldn't see it. Even if I had been able to watch what my heart was doing, it would have done me no good since I was not the one dictating the pace.

People often disparage races like the Sea Otter, saying they are not real mountain bike races because they aren't technical enough. While I would agree that the world's greatest mountain bike races are often technically challenging, I think most of the critics have never actually ridden a course like the Sea Otter's at or anywhere near the speed at which we were attacking it. If I made the smallest bobble or chose a line through a turn that was not 100 percent perfect, I lost a few feet from the contact I had with the rider in front of me. Each time that happened, the fight to regain that few feet drove me deeper into race debt. I was racing nose to tail with the best mountain bike racers of the day, and each of us put a wheel wrong at some point. The effort to regain contact only pushed the pace higher.

I stuck with the leaders until we passed through a small gate that signified the start of the dirt-road climb that would take us back to the Laguna Seca circuit. I was struggling too much, so I decided to back down my effort before the man with the hammer came to visit me. I knew if I were to bonk or blow up I would be left to wander my way around the circuit, embarrassed and broken.

I watched as the leaders rode away from me, certain that each was in his own form of hell but equally certain that there wasn't a thing I could do about it. I plodded along, surprised for a while that no one was passing me. Then, one by one, the best cross-country mountain bike racers in the world began to pass. With each one that went by I felt a new bit of hope, thinking that if I could just stay attached to one of them, or one of the little groups, I could still salvage a top-10 finish. Quickly, though, I started thinking about a top 20. By the time the top 20 was gone, I settled for just connecting with one of the groups so that

I could be paced for the second lap. Unfortunately, each rider to catch me was riding faster than I was able to. It seems that the man with the hammer didn't just appear; he kicked the shit out of me. I made a point of pedaling all the way to the finish, but it was ugly.

Despite this lackluster start to my season, I knew I was riding well enough. With a few tweaks to the training program I would be able to find some good results—maybe even pull off a win or a podium place in one of the World Cup races. DBR was going to send me to Europe to do three rounds of the Grundig World Cup, and I was ecstatic. For me, no matter how cool the mountain bike racing scene was in the United States, nothing could compare with the feeling of racing in Europe. From the fans to the attitude of the other riders, I believed Europe was the place to be to ride a bike. I knew it was also the best place to get competitive race miles in my legs.

In only my second year as a mountain bike racer, I was already starting to become a bit jaded. Many of the American riders were grumbling about the European riders and their drug use. The passive-aggressive mumblings worked their way up the ladder and into the management of NORBA as well. I couldn't argue against the near certainty that some of the Euros were doping with the latest and greatest medical preparations, but I was getting tired of the excuse that the only reason they were faster was because they were doping. It seemed to me that many American mountain bike racers had a misguided notion that riding a mountain bike was much different than riding a road bicycle and that the only way a person could do it well was to live in Marin County, California, or Durango, Colorado.

The riders were complaining, the press was signaling the end of days, and all those who didn't believe there could be performance-enhancing drug use in the professional mountain bike ranks got up on their own soapbox, labeling all of the American cross-country racers lazy and undisciplined. I stood on my own soapbox too. It was clear to me that the main reason for our lack of speed on the World Cup courses was because we weren't training for those races properly, and I let NORBA know it. A mountain bike race at Big Bear or Mammoth, while beautiful and brutal at the same time, was about the worst possible preparation for a World Cup event, I said, since high-altitude races are most often solo tests of climbing, whereas the World Cup races were being battled wheel to wheel and most often at sea level. Of course, the more vehemently I argued my point, the more my views were dismissed.

We departed for Lisbon, Portugal, for the first of my three-race European campaign. I hadn't done much traveling abroad with Americans before. I also didn't know what I should expect from the World Cup. The UCI had added a twist to the World Cup program wherein riders without enough Cup points to qualify for a guaranteed start spot were forced to do a qualifying race before an actual World Cup event, on the same racecourse. Since these qualifiers had fewer riders than the main events, it was pretty easy to ensure a spot in the big show, but the requirement made me nervous, nonetheless. Although I could not find my rhythm on the Lisbon course, I passed the test and was allowed to line up for the real race.

Had I known just how poorly I was going to ride in Lisbon, I think I would have developed a case of the flu, or maybe even fallen back on the dreaded "bad fish for dinner" excuse. On the day of the race I don't think I was even worthy of pinning on a number. I was hardly even a good enough bike racer on that day to ride the 200 or so meters of asphalt that led us from the starting line to the first section of dirt. Plain and simply, I sucked. It seemed as if I had forgotten how to pedal, shift, turn, use my brakes—everything. I'm not sure if it was just the manifestation of my colossal case of nerves or if the food, travel, and sound of the Portuguese language had rendered me stupid. I've had days where I knew things were going to happen before they did, but this was not one of them. In fact, I was so out of sorts that I'm surprised I was even able to find the starting line. Lisbon's course was nontechnical but did require a fair amount of attention and the ability to transition well—the ability to carry speed from one section of trail to the other. Without that important skill, this course consisted of a seemingly endless purgatory of starts and stops. Though I was never confused with Johnny Tomac, I could usually carry decent speed on a course like this, but, temporarily lacking every basic bike riding skill in the book, I was thrown headlong into a torturous couple of hours of hell before calling it a day.

The next stop on the campaign was Houffalize in Belgium. I should have been a dejected puddle of jelly after leaving Lisbon, but the chance to return to my adopted country overcame my dejection over my recent failure. When Alexa and I crossed the border into Belgium, it was all I could do to maintain my composure. I choked back tears with more resolve than I had raced just a couple days earlier. I had, after all, lived in Ursel, Belgium, for more years than I had ever lived in any other place. I was coming home.

The Houffalize qualifier went well. My group was the fastest of the three, and I finished in the top five, so things were looking good for the race. Houffalize is in the Ardennes forest, where the Battle of the Bulge was fought in World War II. I had ridden through it regularly during my road racing career, and now I took the opportunity to venture off on my own to reacquaint myself with the forest's rolling hills and tightly packed villages. We were staying with a couple of other American-based teams in a hotel that was owned by Dutch people. They were happy to speak with me in Nederlands and used me as an interpreter. Even though I was in Wallonie and not my adopted home of East Flanders, I was happy to be *home* for the first time in nearly five years.

The race, however, was a different story. Since I was never even able to see the front, my level of concentration was terrible. I could have been prescribed all the ADHD medication available, but I would still have been lost in a haze of terrible mountain bike racing.

I had only one World Cup race to go, and I had all but written it off before we even crossed the border into Germany. Nonetheless, I went through the motions, pre-riding the course at length and qualifying as seventh-quickest.

Red Bull, the energy drink from Austria, was still a novelty to us Americans—it wasn't even sold in the United States until 1997, and then only in California—but my brief experience with the stuff had suggested that it had magic powers. Since I was having trouble eating anything during races—not to mention that I was riding like I had two wooden legs—I really needed whatever magic I could find, so I bought several cases of Red Bull to use in my race bottles and then to carry back home. I asked Alexa to fill my bottles with straight Red Bull, forgoing any water whatsoever. If Red Bull could do the job for me, I figured I might as well go all the way.

We started on a running track and snaked our way up a little hill onto the long, asphalt straightaway. The wind was blowing from the right, so most of the riders were pinned on the left side of the road. All the years of getting blown all over Belgium and Holland on skinny tires suddenly paid off, and I put in a huge effort, making it into the top 10 riders going into the woods. This was the first time I was actually far enough toward the front of a World Cup to see the lead motorcycle. The first couple of laps were really hard, as I had to settle down from the big effort I'd made at the start, not to mention the fact that we were flying.

We were lapping the course in about 24 minutes, which meant we'd be finished in six laps. By the end of the second lap the front of the race was composed of essentially two small groups, separated by less than a hundred meters. By the fourth lap I had settled down and was starting to think about the finish. I'd always been good at figuring out the worst possible placing I could get out of any breakaway I ever found myself in. In other words, I can count.

On lap five I started thinking about the effort it was going to take to get across the gap and into that front group. As it sat, the best I was going to be able to pull off was 7th place. I was feeling pretty good. The Red Bull was working like a champ. We seemed to be taking some ground back from the front riders, so I decided to wait until halfway through the last lap before mounting an extra effort.

Crossing the line on the bell lap, I was thinking about a podium. All I had to do was put in one massive 20-something-minute effort and keep it on two wheels and I would put the United States back on the World Cup map. I thought about where on the course I might zip up my jersey. I wondered if my shades were clean enough. I needed to look good for the photos, right?

I grabbed a bottle from Alexa in the feed zone that was situated at the beginning of the road section. I went to toss one of the empties but was surprised to find it still full. I grabbed the other one. It was full too. I'd been too busy racing to look after my fueling. I took a quick sip from the new bottle and tossed it aside. I looked forward as we made it to the top of a little rise to try to figure out what was going on with those front-runners. I decided I should shuffle myself to the front of our little group, so I pushed on the pedals a bit harder. Nothing happened. Shit. I grabbed one of my bottles and tried to squeeze some of the sweet, energy-filled goodness down my throat. I needed some Red Bull magic—fast. But I was too late; the engine was already sputtering. Visions of the podium and sprays of champagne changed to thoughts of a footnote marking my top-20 finish.

It was a lot worse than that, though. By the end of the road section I couldn't hold on to the wheel in front of me. All those years of experience hiding from the wind weren't helping in the least. I was the last of our group to roll into the dirt, and when I did it seemed to suck my wheels deep into it. My bike felt like the brakes were rubbing. I thought I had a flat tire. I thought my frame was cracked. I thought the bottom bracket had seized.

Bonk. The man with the hammer hit me hard, and I started to slow down as if I had just released the parachute. What was worse, he came out of nowhere, without warning.

I started getting passed. Numbers flashed through my head—finishing position numbers. "Okay, top 30," I tried to convince myself. St. Wendel's course was not terribly technical, but it was becoming increasingly difficult for me to negotiate any of the small roots, rocks, or log crossings. My arms were weak, and my legs were getting close to worthless. I'd been rolling along all day in the big ring but now was forced to roll my left hand forward and accept the middle one. Seemingly every 50 meters or so, I was looking for an easier gear in the back.

Have you ever been so drunk that you know what is going on around you, if ever so slightly, but you can't do anything about it? You know what you want to say, but no intelligible words will come out? You try to go straight, but all you can do is weave? That was me. I had left some dimwitted copilot in charge of my body, and he had none of the same goals I did.

I finally made it to the finish. The last half of the course had taken its toll, and I had tipped over a couple times. I'd resorted to the small ring and one of the three biggest cogs in the back, so when I say "tipped over," I mean just that. I was more than 40 minutes behind the winner. At the beginning of the last 20-something-minute lap I had been with the leaders, and now I was more than 40 minutes behind. I'll let you do the math.

I probably should have been more dejected than I was, but I was surprisingly okay —after the initial realization of what had just happened, of course. Maybe it was just too many years of self-imposed lack of oxygen to the brain, but I wrote off my race as a learning experience and vowed to adjust both my training and my in-race caloric intake to keep this sort of thing from happening again.

Back in the States, my next real mission was the penultimate Olympic qualifying race in Conyers, Georgia, on the actual 1996 Olympic mountain bike course. The folks at USA Cycling had shown me power output data for the course, and I had been training with that race in mind ever since the camp in Alpine.

A couple laps of this course, which was located in what would be the equestrian park for the Olympics, assured me that my preparation had not been wasted. The Conyers course had nothing in terms of extended climbing and was not terribly technical either, but it was one of those courses that would rise up and bite you in the ass as soon as you started to have any problems or became tired.

Since this race counted as an Olympic qualifier, we lined up based upon our accumulated Olympic qualifying points. As soon as the gun went off, the race seemed to sort itself out, at least for the early going. Tinker quickly established a lead, and Johnny Tomac, Rishi Grewal, and I formed a disheveled chase. Rishi's laps were hot and cold. For a while he was with us, then he was behind us. He would catch and then miss a shift, causing him to fall behind again. Johnny T. might have been saving himself for the final, but I still felt like I was stronger than he was on the little climbs and other power sections. Our race was very much a yo-yo match, though. He would ride the terraced descent faster than I and establish a little lead, and then I would catch and pass him where power was needed.

After a couple laps of this game, I decided that staying with him was not the best strategy; even if I were stronger than he, the constant passing under power would do nothing but waste energy. I opted to keep him in sight and watch his moves but refrain from racing him until the last lap or so.

Instead I was reunited with Rishi Grewal. I'd known Rishi for more than a year now and found him to be one of the funnier bike racers I'd ever met. Rishi had a more insane and blue-collar outlook toward bike racing than most of the other guys I knew; he was almost Belgian from that standpoint. He wasn't overly analytical and didn't possess the sense of entitlement I was used to seeing in so many other American cyclists. Like his brother Alexi, who won the road race gold medal in the 1984 Los Angeles Olympic Games, Rishi was hyperfocused and an incredibly talented bike racer. On a good day both Grewals were absolute geniuses when it came to turning over the pedals. But unfortunately, both brothers could have bad days that would have taken them out of contention at a kindergarten bike rodeo.

The two of us attacked the course together almost as if we were teammates. Unfortunately for Rishi, he kept having problems with his shifters. He'd surge ahead and then fall behind as he tried to find a gear. As we climbed out of the back side of the course toward the finish, the straw broke the camel's back. Rishi was leading me when his shift went south once again.

"I've had enough of your shit," he screamed at his bike as he threw it on the ground, pointing his finger at it as if it were a not-yet-housebroken puppy. "Whore!"

His tantrum was so completely out of place and absurdly animated that I started laughing in between giant gulps of air.

I crossed the finish line solidly in 3rd place with just three laps to go, but I was biding my time and eyeballing the leaders in front of me. I watched my heart rate monitor when I could, doing my best to keep it close to 176 beats per minute. I drank as much fluid as I could swallow and ate as much as I could stomach.

Perhaps it was payback from laughing at Rishi, but on this new lap, as I approached the spot where he had disparaged his bike, I felt the rear tire of my bike going flat. This was not going to be good. I slowed down a bit to sort myself out. Holding my position was going to require a superquick tire change and then a hard chase. But there was another problem: The front was going flat as well. I crept to the top of the climb before attempting the fix.

I attacked the front first, pulling the partially inflated inner tube from my jersey's middle pocket. I ripped the old tube from the tire, stuffed the new one in, and then twisted the air cartridge open, inflating the tube the rest of the way. I reinstalled the front wheel and then went for the rear. By this time in my mountain bike career I was reasonably quick at changing flats, so the old tube was out and the new one in place in less than a minute. I threaded another air cartridge onto the adapter, pushed the Presta valve into it, and cracked open the flow of air for a second time. But this time I hadn't seated the tire bead properly and the tube was trying to escape the confines of the rim and tire.

"Shit!"

I partially deflated the tube and reseated the tire. I connected the cartridge again and gave it a twist to start the flow of air, but there wasn't enough left. I believe I was probably one of the only pros in the world to carry a third air cartridge, and I was happy to have it. Once again I repeated the ritual and gave the full contents of the cartridge to the tube. I watched carefully to make sure the bead stayed seated. I collected myself and climbed back on my bike to rejoin the race. Rider upon rider had gone by, so I was definitely back to at least 20th place at this point. I jumped on the pedals, but in only a few yards I realized that something had gone seriously wrong. Somehow in my haste to complete the repair and get back on the bike, I had managed to puncture this last remaining tube. An Olympic berth, which had once been a decent possibility, now had long-shot odds, like a horse only an idiot would bet on. A four-dollar tube was the culprit that dashed a year's worth of preparation and close to a lifetime of Olympic dreaming.

There was only one race left to determine the two men and two women who would represent the United States in the first-ever mountain bike race at the Olympic games. I got over being grumpy and decided to soldier on with my training and go for it anyway. A podium finish would have been a nice statement, but unless just about everyone ahead of me retired from cycling, I was almost certainly not going to Atlanta.

This last race on the Olympic selection calendar was the spot of my semibreakthrough performance from 1995, Traverse City, Michigan. It was a good course for me, with short climbs, lots of trees, and thick sea-level air.

But when I arrived at the race venue, my mood immediately started to sour. All the efforts from the team staff seemed to be directed toward ensuring that Susan was happy. I understood the motivation to do everything possible to make her race as worry-free as it could be, but the atmosphere in the team was almost aggressive. I felt like a teenager trying to get backstage for a rock-and-roll show, with the bouncer shoving me out of the way and telling me to beat it. The bouncer in this case was Bryan Seti.

Things got worse the evening before the race, when, after my massage, I realized that all the team vehicles were gone and the restaurant at the venue was closed. I knocked on doors for a while to no avail and then started thinking about the worst-case scenario: pizza. I wandered around a bit more and eventually was able to bum a couple of Styrofoam bowls of cereal. Pissed off, I went to bed.

Race day started with an even more insulting slap in the face. Seti had decided it would be the best thing for Sue to have every one of us at the DBR truck for her entire warm-up and other pre-race preparations. It was as if he wanted us to become a group of cheerleaders, jumping and applauding the fact that our sweet little Suzy had finally learned how to use the potty. I wanted to kill the man. Interestingly enough, so did Sue. She had, after all, gotten ready for plenty of races in her time. She knew the drill. And like most other athletes I have known, she didn't want to be interrupted or bothered in her pre-race routine. I sat next to the well-worn box van for what seemed like an eternity before eventually calling foul, breaking the chain of command, and walking away so that I could prepare for my own race.

In front of my Michigan-native mom, my Aunt Peggy, and my Uncle Russ, I was extremely proud to be called to the line: I was still worthy of a mention in the race for a spot on the first mountain bike Olympic team. But that was where pride, motivation, loyalty, and any sort of ability to suffer for both my employer and myself completely left my body. The gun went off, and I went through the motions for less than a quarter of a lap before climbing off my bike and hurling it into the trees. It was a culmination of the resentment that had been mounting, in my mind, against Seti. As a former athlete, Bryan should have known that the day-of-race preparation is a ritual as sacred as that in any place of worship. I had gone to great lengths to make sure everything was perfect for my own race, but that had all been taken away. Elite-level athletes are sometimes fragile creatures, and I certainly proved on more than one occasion that I was not exempt from that rule. Unfortunately, this time I presented that characteristic in an embarrassingly glaring fashion. I turned around and headed back to the DBR truck. Capping the day, no one was home in the DBR camp, and the keys to my room were locked inside our box van. It was no real surprise that I wasn't offered a contract with Diamondback for 1997, and that was just fine with me.

8

CHEQUAMEGON

MY 1996 SEASON, WHICH HAD STARTED WITH SO MUCH HOPE, WAS going nowhere. I knew I was not going to be on the Diamondback team in 1997, but I was in negotiations with Charles Aaron, who was running the Ross/Jeep program, and the prospect of landing a ride on his team was motivating. Despite the bad rides I'd been turning in for Diamondback, my fitness level was, amazingly, still quite good, and since I was not going to the World Championships, I set my sights firmly on winning my second Chequamegon 40.

By 1996 only one rider had won the Chequamegon 40 twice: Greg LeMond. I'd won the 1992 event, and my friend Geno Oberpriller had taken home the trophy in '93. In '94 I was definitely strong enough and believe I would have won by a huge margin if I had not double-flatted and then turned in close to the slowest tire repair in bike racing history. I had missed the event in 1995 because I had been representing the United States at the World Mountain Bike Championships. It was time to win again.

My preparation for Chequamegon didn't include anything out of the ordinary. I stuck with my normal schedule of racing as much as possible, which included weeknight road criteriums, mountain bike races, track races, and whatever road or mountain bike race I could get to on the weekends. The "40" is a fast, rolling race that favors a strong rider. Admittedly it is nothing like some of the epic, all-mountain-style races that take place out West, but at race-winning speed there are plenty of sections on the Chequamegon course that can cause crashes if not ridden with skill. There aren't any places to hide either, so if a rider starts to come apart, the wheels come off the wagon in a hurry. Chasing back through groups of riders in the 1994 event, I had witnessed more than one otherwise strong rider who appeared to be dragging a 500-pound anchor.

I heard that Trek Factory rider Jeff Bicknell was going to be there, and my friend Bob Roll was in too. He had called to see if he could bum a ride with me to Hayward, Wisconsin, and back. Of course I had no problem chauffeuring Bob, nor was I averse to having some time to hang out with him again. The last time I'd had him in my car we had gone to see a weekday matinee of the David Lynch film *Blue Velvet*. Not surprisingly, we were the only two people in the Walnut Creek, California, theater. After the movie Bob wanted to drive around the neighborhoods blasting Metallica loud enough to be heard all the way to San Francisco.

The level of competition Bicknell and Roll would present was a complete coin toss. I knew Bicknell to be strong, as I had raced head to head with him on numerous occasions in the California State Series. Racing against Bob, on the other hand, was more of a mystery. I'd seen him do absolutely astonishing things in the Belgian cold, rain, and wind. If he had his mind set upon it, he might just ride my legs off and leave me for the bears.

I picked Bob up at the Minneapolis–Saint Paul International Airport, and the next day we made the three-hour drive to Hayward. Bob was being hosted, so, as his driver, I was to be hosted as well. Hayward is not a big town, but for most of the year hotel rooms are available if not plentiful. However, when you descend upon the area with more than 2,500 mountain bikers and their entourages, rooms become scarce in a hurry. I was relieved to have a place to stay.

I was also happy to have a premium starting position. The Chequamegon promoter, Gary Crandall, always roped off space at the start line for roughly a hundred spots, which he filled with elite racers, former winners, and a select few VIPs. Thus, Bob and I didn't have to join the cattle call of riders who started lining up in the wee hours of the morning as if they were trying to get concert tickets. Instead we were able to warm up a little, and I was able to fit in time for my customary hundred pre-race trips to pee before forcing myself to the front of the line, just behind the lead ATV.

In the start everything went according to my plan. The gun went off, and, as I had done in '92, I began my impersonation of a *keirin* rider, sweeping my bike back and forth behind the ATV so no one else could join me in its draft. We rolled a short distance down Main Street, made the left onto Highway 63, and then turned right on Highway 77. My legs were easily able to follow the lead ATV's little accelerations, which I knew was a good sign. The giant peloton increased its speed as it made the gentle climb up Heartbreak Hill, named for the deadly toll it had taken on logging horses when the road iced over in the days before horses were traded for trucks. As soon as the entrance to Rosie's Field became clear, the ATV sped up and the race was officially on.

Despite the Chequamegon course being conducive to road racing tactics, my plan was the same each year: Go as hard as I could from the start to shake the tree, then continue on. With so many people vying for the same bit of ground, the best place to be was in front of the fray. Once I'd entered the field and my bike was clearly pointed toward the finish in Cable, I put my head down, grabbed the biggest gear I could turn over with any degree of efficiency, turned my brain off, and pedaled. Shortly after the start the lead group whittled down to just Bicknell and me.

Bicknell was matching my effort pedal stroke for pedal stroke, which made me a little nervous. Jeff was a better climber than I; that didn't mean much in the Chequamegon forest, but since we seemed to be equally strong in the opening stages, any little bobble on my part could prove to be a death blow to my shot at a second victory.

As we neared the halfway point it seemed clear that one of us would go home with the win, barring some sort of catastrophe. Shortly before the steep climb to the top of the Seeley Fire Tower Hill, Jeff was on the wrong end of catastrophe.

"I've got a flat," he announced.

"Awww, man . . ." was my only reply.

There are two types of bike racers: those who find great strength in the face of a setback such as a flat or crash and those who crack because of it. I didn't know Jeff well enough to anticipate how he would respond to his flat, but I didn't want to take any chances. As soon as I knew I was out of sight of my breakaway partner, I shifted into an even taller gear and began my individual time trial toward the finish.

The foremost advantage to leading this race was the constant company of Mike Cooper, the ATV driver. He was never close enough to reward me with shelter from the wind, but simply having someone in front of me to act as a course guide was a great comfort. I could stare at the quad and pedal without even thinking about the course. Had Mike not been in front of me at the approach to the Fire Tower Hill, I surely would have blown through the course tape that marked the turn off the trail and onto the climb.

As I began the climb, the toll of my big-gear, do-or-die solo time trial effort became instantly evident as even the muscles in my neck screamed in protest. The ascent to the Seeley Fire Tower stair-steps its way upward, with steep pitches followed by short, flat sections. Each steep section requires so much effort that the little bit of flat that follows feels like riding in quicksand. I crested the top, knowing I'd gone faster on previous trips, and was happy to be done with it.

A long logging-road descent followed, so I took the brief opportunity to suck down some of the contents of my water bottle and shove some food from my jersey pockets into my mouth. This would be the last good section of the course on which to grab food, and the absolute last thing I needed was to bonk and start firing on only three cylinders. I managed to choke down the last bit of food I would touch just before turning right off the logging road onto the American Birkebeiner cross-country ski trail.

When most riders speak of this race, they allude to the fire-tower climb as the pivotal point of the race. Though the ability to stay on the bike all the way to the top definitely allows a faster ascent than climbing on foot, the section of Birkebeiner trail I was just entering is really the most crucial section of the course. I would soon know exactly how much gas I had left in the tank because the trail's undulating terrain would tell me instantly if I was still going fast enough to win. Traveling fast over the short, continuous power hills of the Birkebeiner trail requires a rider to crest each little rise with enough speed and energy to continue down the back side without any hesitation. At the bottom of each dip I would need to power out of the trough and up the next hill, downshifting no more than one gear toward the top. If I lost my timing or my legs ran out of power, I would end up struggling up each hill and then slowly coasting down. Luckily for me, my rhythm in the power-sapping rollers was spot-on, and I checked this critical section off my list.

The last section of trees that marks the entrance to the World Cup Trail was the most beautiful thing I had ever seen. I ducked into the trees and enjoyed an instant drop in temperature. This part of the course is definitely the most fun, and even with screaming legs I enjoyed flowing through the trees at speed.

If I had been a race car, the engineers in the pits would have been wringing their hands at this point, hoping I could get to the finish under my own power. The low fuel light was fully illuminated, my legs were beginning to telegraph the telltale signs of cramps on the horizon, and my vision was becoming more than a little impaired. But I had just one short section of false flat across a field of power-sucking dead grass and a short climb before the descent to the finish. I fought with the bike across the face of the hill and turned upward. The short climb through dead grass and sand drained what was left in the tank, and at the top everything went black. If the slightest gust of wind had hit me at that moment, I would have tipped over, and I doubt I could have found the strength to even unclip from my pedals. I quite literally could see nothing for a few seconds. But once the world started pointing downhill, my vision returned and my legs agreed to keep turning the pedals over.

The feeling of wind on my face as I descended toward the finish line tipped a tiny bit of fuel back into my tank. I ventured a quick peek over my shoulder to see if anyone was close and, seeing no one, allowed myself a little smile. I made it to the bottom of the descent, downshifted, negotiated the big left-hander, grunted up the little rise toward the finish, and claimed my second Chequamegon victory. I had nothing left as I crossed the line. I couldn't even remove my helmet.

Jeff Bicknell, who'd fixed his flat quickly and chased to within just under a minute, missed a crucial turn at the bottom of the descent and ended up in the parking lot before sorting himself out and finding the course again. Jeff's bobble allowed Bob to sneak in ahead of him.

It was one of my proudest performances on the bike, yet the victory was bittersweet. I was not the strongest rider in the race, just the most motivated on the day. I threw all my cards on the table and walked away with the win. I honestly believe I could have taken on any of the world's best mountain bike riders of the time and still come out on top. All the same, it was a bit too little, too late. Had I ridden with that much defiant anger and motivation in the final Olympic qualifier, I might have marched in the opening ceremony of the 1996 Olympic games. As bike racers we all too often look at race wins as stepping-stones toward something else—something life-changing, perhaps. In reality, it seems that the experience of racing itself is the important part.

Bob and I stuck around for the awards ceremony that evening, where I collected a custom-made plaque and a Trek mountain bike for the overall win. After talking with a few friends and shaking some hands, Bobke and I loaded our stuff into the back of my truck and headed back to Minneapolis.

9

OOOOH, BARRACUDA

I'D KNOWN CHARLES AARON SINCE I HAD FIRST RETURNED TO THE
United States. He was a local road racer with aspirations of running a professional road team. In 1996 Charles was hired by Ross/
Jeep to run their mountain bike program after having proven
himself capable by running a regional road racing team. At first
it was a bit of a stretch for the Baltimore resident because try
as he might, the allure of mountain bike racing was a bit lost on
him; he was more interested in the road side of cycling.

Nevertheless, while his team was nowhere near the same level
as the mighty Volvo/Cannondale, GT Bicycles, or Diamondback
squads of the day, his riders were getting reasonable results, their
bikes seemed to work, and they seemed to be getting paid. As
much as I would have liked to stay on board with KK, I was quite

certain I was going to be axed from DBR, so I started talking with Charles about racing for his program much earlier in the season than I normally would have.

Our courtship continued throughout the season until finally we were able to come to an agreement and get the paperwork sorted out. The contract was quite a step back from where I had been with Diamondback. My 1996 contract, though paltry in comparison to what many other riders were making, was worth $35,000 plus some readily attainable bonuses. My new contract moved me back to $20,000 and an all-but-nonexistent bonus schedule. I was okay with it, though; I only wanted a chance to race my bike and—I hoped—to feel that my efforts were worthwhile.

Charles and I continued to talk frequently throughout the fall and winter, and I really appreciated the fact that he found my experience helpful. I was also full of spite against the program I was leaving—the one that had turned its back on me—and I wanted to prove I could rise to a higher level once again.

After following an actual training program in 1996 and (despite some setbacks) seeing what it could accomplish, I concentrated seriously on my off-season program, incorporating in-line speed skating, cross-country skiing, and some limited weight training. I was determined to increase my leg power to compensate for my severe lack of lung power at the higher-altitude races. I continued to ride my trainer, looking forward to the day when I would be able to ride outside and, better yet, race.

I was invited to race the Redlands Classic stage race with a version of Team Dirt, a road team assembled from a motley group of mountain bike racers. Redlands was the first big national race of the season, but this year, for the first time, I was looking at it as nothing more than a training ride; there was no reason to believe I would come up with any sort of good result.

Redlands was the only race I had ever entered that provided host housing for all competitors. Even when I had ridden for the Coors Light squad, we had stayed in host housing. Staying in a complete stranger's house with one or more other bike racers is a strange experience. Sharing meals, a living room, television, and bathrooms with entire families or retired couples is uncomfortable, no matter how you slice it. Part of me always felt obliged to hang out and chat with the hosts, although I typically wanted nothing other than to turn my brain off and put my feet up.

For the 1997 event I was assigned another ex–road racer turned mountain biker, Paul Willerton, as a roommate. I had first met Paul in 1991 at a race in France when he was racing for Greg LeMond's Z team. In 1994 he defected to the off-road side of professional cycling and pulled off a stellar performance at the World Mountain Bike Championships in Vail, finishing 4th. Although just out of medal contention, his ride in Vail had opened Haro Bicycles' coffers, and Paul had signed a three-year deal. Unfortunately, injury and illness had put a damper on the performances that both Paul and Haro were expecting, and the company had stopped paying him.

Paul seemed to be searching for some reason to keep racing. By all accounts I should have been in the same situation, but I was still trying to crack the mountain bike nut and was determined to keep trying.

"Why do you think you keep doing this?" Paul asked me suddenly. "What keeps you coming back?"

"I haven't won anything big yet," I responded without even thinking.

It was the first time I'd ever spoken those words—perhaps even the first time I'd formulated the thought. As a young pro in Europe, my ability to continue on was based on my desire to discover what I could accomplish as a bike racer. As time rolled on and I learned that I could control races and ride well, really well, in the service of the sport's great riders, my focus shifted from wanting to see what could be to simply wanting to be the greatest domestique I could possibly be. The switch to mountain bikes had given me something else to focus on and a new cycling discipline to learn, but it had also brought me back mentally to 1988, when everything was shiny and new and my career was full of nothing but hope. I spent my first two years on the fat tires seeing glimmers of hope, despite some stumbles along the way. Although my new team was a step back from the Diamondback program, I was finding new motivation, even if that determination was tempered by some last-chance panic.

Unfortunately, my time at Redlands didn't get me closer to my goal. In the race's first stage I managed to get tangled up in a fairly ugly crash. It was caused the same way most crashes are: A rider went into a corner too fast, ran out of talent, and took a few people down in the process. After I checked my limbs and determined that I was not paralyzed, a momentary bit of confusion ensued. Instead of soldiering on, I climbed into the back of one of the neutral support vehicles and was taken to the circuit's start/finish line. Although I knew the rules and knew there was no way I would be allowed to start the next morning, I argued my case anyway. But that was it—I was out of the race before it had really started.

Next on the agenda was the Cactus Cup, which for several years had served as the official kickoff to the mountain bike season. My prior two outings at West World in Scottsdale, Arizona, had proved less than pleasing, so I decided to look at this year's Cactus Cup as another low-key training race. I kept my expectations low and used the race to build fitness for the second event of the season, the Sea Otter Classic.

Sea Otter was going to be a challenge for my Nautilus Nutritionals—Barracuda team. Our small squad was a fairly strange band of characters, misfits in many ways who were too good to be written off completely but not quite good enough to be part of a bigger, better program. We arrived in Monterey early in the week and were able to spend time getting to know one another.

Jeff Bicknell had spent the previous two years racing for the Trek Factory team with Travis Brown and 1996 Olympian Don Myrah. I had raced with Jeff, a tall, soft-spoken Californian, in the California State Championship Series in '95 and '96. He and I had been the two protagonists at the Chequamegon 40 the fall before we became teammates. Jeff and I were similar riders and hit it off immediately.

Lisa Sher was our team's only downhill racer as well as its only female. Like Bicknell and me, Lisa had knocked on the door of success but had never seen it completely through. We went on to become good friends.

Although I wasn't familiar with his name, I remember seeing another teammate, Mike Janelle, at races in previous years. Janelle was one of many talented riders whom I saw over the course of my cycling career who might have been much more successful if he could have toned down the intensity of his training. He was one of those riders who has just one speed—wide open. It didn't matter if it was the day before the race, three days before the race, or the race itself—Janelle rode as hard as he could.

The downside was that his top speed was negatively affected by the fact that he could never ride slowly. If Nautilus-Barracuda had been a road team, I would have had to kill Mike because he wouldn't have been able to ride as a true teammate. As it was, the guy was hilarious, and I liked having him around for comic relief, if nothing else.

Rounding out our squad was Matt O'Keefe, a former collegiate hockey player who had found cycling and worked his way up the ladder quickly. He was a sponge for cycling knowledge and attacked his training and racing with a lot of focus. Matt also had a completely warped sense of humor that often caught us completely off guard.

I was happy to be returning to Laguna Seca and the Sea Otter Classic. This race's cruel joke is that you have to be prepared for every possible type of weather. It doesn't matter that you're too hot today because tomorrow could bring freezing rain and gale-force winds. I love racing with the possibility of those conditions looming overhead.

I was coming to Sea Otter with a race plan, which, for me, was a big departure. For most of my career, whether I was at the top of my game or not, I would simply take each race as it was presented to me, hoping something good might develop, that I might be able to take home a stage win or wind up with a favorable ranking in the overall classification. While riding for the Diamondback team the year before, I'd come to this race with strong form and should have been able to finish in the top 10 overall, but instead I'd fallen flat on my face. This year I knew from my result at the Cactus Cup that my form still had a ways to go, so for Sea Otter I set my sights solely on the dirt criterium.

I limped through the opening time trial stage and then began to prepare for the short-course crit. During my first year with Diamondback I had ridden the Tioga Tension Disc rear wheel as often as I could; I absolutely loved it. The tension disc was made up of a webbing of Kevlar bands loosely encased in a Mylar cover and laced to a conventional hub and rim. Although disc wheels had been used in road racing since the mid-'80s to decrease aerodynamic drag, the Tioga disc wasn't really about an aerodynamic advantage. Instead, since the Kevlar bands acted as spokes, the wheel provided a cushioning effect that reduced the harshness of impacts with rocks, roots, and other big hits to the back wheel. Since the wheel also provided some lateral flex, I found that I was able to load it coming into a corner and let it push the bike out of the corner as the wheel attempted to spring back into shape. Best of all, the wheel made an incredible rumbling noise that was amplified by its drum-like sides and announced your presence to everyone around.

Although my time trial performance wasn't the best of my life, I'd done well enough to be called to the criterium starting line within striking distance of the front rows. When the gun went off, I went as hard as I could go for two laps, disc rumbling behind. I quickly passed enough people to put me in the front of the race. Short-course, wheel-to-wheel racing has always been very motivating for me, and within another lap I had recovered from the early effort and was ready to think about playing to win.

As short as this race was, I fully expected the feeling of reprieve wouldn't last very long and that I'd soon be back in full suffering mode. As the first little test attacks came from other riders in the front, reacting to them took more out of me than

I had anticipated. My legs felt heavy and sluggish—almost blocked. It wasn't uncommon for me to feel like that over such a short distance, but I had warmed up well and had made it through the effort of the first few laps without any problem, so the current state of affairs was confusing.

Knowing another increase of speed would be coming soon, I tried to make my way back to the front of the group but wasn't able to make any headway. In an instant my desire to win the stage diminished to simply wanting to finish in the front group. As soon as the next attack was launched, though, I found myself struggling to maintain contact. I pushed as hard on the pedals as I possibly could, but with each pedal stroke I felt as if the resistance was higher. Riders who didn't seem to be working hard at all were passing me now. Even the most gradual rise felt like climbing a wall. I started thinking there might actually be something seriously physically wrong with me, so I decided to stop at the top of the course and take inventory of my body. I crested the top of the little climb and stopped pedaling. The bike almost instantly stopped rolling. The feeling was so weird that I got off the bike to take a look and immediately saw that the rear wheel had pulled so far to one side that I could barely get it to turn by hand. My newly built disc had lost tension on one side, and the rim was rubbing against the brake. I should have been mad, but in fact I was relieved to know the problem was with the bike, not my legs.

After a bad showing at the NORBA National Championship Series (NCS) events in 1996, I was determined to find a way to perform better at the high-altitude races. Since the first NCS race was in Big Bear, California, I decided to go acclimate to the 7,000-plus-foot elevation's thin air. Big Bear's course was never one to suit me, but if I could limit my losses there and finish in the top 30 or 40, my position on the starting line for subsequent NCS events would be better. Jeff Bicknell, who lived in Big Bear, agreed to let me stay with him for the three weeks before the race.

I loaded my double-wide bike bag with my road and mountain bikes and made my way to Southern California for three weeks of focused training near the racecourse. I had tried this approach before with only marginal results, so while I didn't think I would be developing a completely new body in three weeks, I did hope to further my high-elevation riding education. For me, the slow-motion feeling of riding at high altitude was as much a challenge as the rarefied air. Because I had competed in hundreds of bicycle races at sea level but only about 30 at high altitude, I tended to attack harder than my already challenged red blood cells could handle. My sea-level engine would blow up, and I would cough and sputter along like an old man.

Big Bear's course was one of my least favorites to race, but I loved being there to train. Just being on different terrain was motivating, and Jeff and I pieced together some fantastic rides. We lived the monastic life of professional cyclists, eating, training, and sleeping in the correct amounts. Even so, after three weeks of high-altitude training, I was no closer to thinking I was a high-altitude racer.

Big Bear also marked the first race during which I paid special attention to our downhiller teammate, Lisa. Because the gravity events were held on Saturday and the cross-country on Sunday, my Saturdays were always free. I liked riding hard the day before a race to blow out the cobwebs, but never for much more than an hour or two. Lisa had asked for a little training advice and also for some help with her pre-race warm-up routine. Downhillers are really the sprinters of mountain bike racing, and since I had spent much of my European career riding in the service of road sprinters, I could always identify with their mountain bike counterparts. In many cases I felt more akin to the elite downhillers than to my fellow endurance riders. The good downhillers possess a cockiness that can both charm and intimidate. They have bike-handling skills that normal people cannot even comprehend. But most are easily as fragile as their counterparts on the road, and Lisa was no exception.

Listening to Lisa try to find the secret to success reminded me of myself. She had all the basic tools she needed to win, and she deserved to finish on the podium, but some elusive ingredient was lacking. I had no surefire way of helping her find it, but I thought if I could at least be there to make sure she was calm and confident before her races, she might have a chance.

Lisa had another major obstacle standing in the way of her success. The team management and mechanics, who'd begun the season with only nominal patience for her, had long since given up trying to help her. Compared with the road racers and cross-country mountain bike racers that they'd become accustomed to dealing with, a single downhiller seemed to require as much attention as an entire road team. The equipment, though developing quickly, was still archaic, and the mechanics had to do a lot of work each day to make sure that her bikes worked as intended. In addition, whereas a mechanic's duties regarding cross-country bikes were mostly limited to cleaning, lubing, adjusting, and tightening, a downhill bike required about the same amount of attention as a race car. Lisa's bike needed nearly a complete overhaul after every run, and the suspension settings needed to be monitored, adjusted, and modified.

Our Big Bear experience began with a road ride around the lake in which I pretended to be the derny motor pacer and Lisa the six-day rider. She followed the proper "ja" protocol to speed me up and the "ohhh" to slow me down. It was an incredible sensation that made me feel like I was back in Europe and the sprint was approaching.

Once back at the race venue, we collected her extra clothing, a pump, some tubes, and a stationary trainer so she could warm up at the top of the mountain. A mechanic rightly should have ridden the chairlift to the top with Lisa, but all of the mechanical skills I lacked were offset by the fact that I viewed her as a friend, not an enemy.

I think if Lisa had known that seating myself in a chairlift was as comforting a feeling for me as having my teeth drilled, she would have released me from active duty. But I kept quiet about that, and we made it to the top of the mountain without incident.

After every one of the pro women had exited the start house and finished the course, Lisa took home 3rd place. It was a breakthrough that sparked a burst of momentum that would carry her through the rest of a pretty successful season. Bike racing is funny like that—riders often need only the slightest bit of encouragement to find the podium, and once they find it, most keep hitting the podium steps again and again thereafter. All I contributed to Lisa's day was a friendly ear and two hands to carry some gear, yet it felt like a *team* to me, a really good feeling.

The marketing department from our sponsor, Nautilus Nutritionals, had come out to see the race and get a firsthand idea of what other sponsors were doing in the sport of mountain bike racing. In addition to the marketers, they also brought along one of their dietitians so that she might better understand the needs of the team. From a racer's perspective, the Nautilus staff were good sponsors to deal with because they mostly stayed out of the way. When they did ask questions, it felt like they were simply clarifying something about which they already had a fair understanding. Despite that feeling, I reacted to the dietitian's advice about the plain bean burrito I ate for lunch the day before the race as if she were offering me a case of the plague.

True to the form I had grown accustomed to at high-altitude races, I sucked. My bike, although less than desirable in many ways, was not the culprit. Over and over I replayed the days, weeks, months, and years that had come before this one race to try to find an answer to my problem. I replayed every inch of the race itself, looking for an answer. This was my third consecutive trip to Big Bear, and the fact that a mid-50s finish was the best I'd ever done in the event slapped me in the face. I made up my mind to hate high altitude in the same way that it apparently hated me.

With all the Nautilus folks still in town, we decided to have a little impromptu party at Bicknell's house. Parties that are primarily made up of cross-country mountain bike racers have never been known to reach rock-and-roll proportions, but we did our best, and it turned out that our guests were even lighter-weight drinkers than we were. A few 12-packs of Mexican beer were all it took for the party to get sloppy and drag on into the wee hours of the morning.

As my own beer consumption had stopped hours earlier, I was tagged to be the official driver down the mountain and to the airport. Charles and the women from Nautilus were either unfamiliar with the route or were in no condition to be driving. We loaded ourselves into the little rental car, and before I even had a chance to start it Charles tossed out a dare.

"I bet you can't make me carsick."

"You didn't really just say that, did you?" I was incredulous. But Charles just giggled. "I'll go ahead and let you retract that," I told him.

I'd been up and down the mountain on a bike and in cars more times than I cared to remember. Moreover, over the years I had learned how to descend a mountain by car from some of the world's greatest soigneurs—people who often take death-defying, thrill-ride risks in order to get the best spot at the next feed zone. I was not about to risk a car full of people I hardly knew to win a bet with a friend, but I was also not about to let him get away completely unscathed.

The top part of the mountain doesn't offer much opportunity for carsick-inducing driving, but after a few miles the constantly winding road is the perfect playground. I overshot the entrance to each turn and then attempted to hit the apex, causing the tires on the little rental to squeal with disapproval. Instead of then straightening out the steering wheel, I kept the turn in until the car was touching the lane lines, and then I overcorrected in the other direction. In other words, for each turn I snapped the wheel four times so that my passengers' inner ears would communicate with the contents of their stomachs. Less than halfway down the mountain, Charles had had enough. He continued on foot while the rest of us got a cup of coffee. Needless to say, I won the bet.

Legend has it that in the twilight of his career the great Eddy Merckx was so afflicted with an obsessive desire to fidget with his seat position that his team mechanics were ordered to keep tools out of his reach. While there are painfully few similarities between the Cannibal and me, we definitely shared this bad habit. A rider in form can comfortably ride just about any bike. The seat position can be wrong, the handlebars can be too small—it really doesn't matter. A rider in form simply gets on and goes because the feeling of *form*—the perfect combination of physical and emotional fitness—creates an almost euphoric state in which the pain and suffering of racing a bike become life-giving, and equipment hindrances cease to even register. A rider in form can crash, get up, and chase for as long as it takes, while one without form will never progress beyond staring at the torn handlebar tape.

My high-altitude phobia was developing its own heartbeat at this point. I bought an ionizer to take with me to Mammoth in the hope that it might create a more sea level–like environment for sleeping. In addition to looking for the cure for bike racing deficiency at high altitude in self-help books and electronic gadgets, I began losing faith in every component on my bike except the pedals, tires, and brakes, all products I had specifically requested. The Shock Works suspension forks we were using had let me down for the last time, so I enlisted the help of my friend Mark Zeh to source Shock Works decals for my old Manitou 4 fork, in an attempt at disguise. Although bicycle suspension was still a ways from genius, by 1997 the Manitou 4 was about as cutting-edge as an eight-track tape player. Compared to the Shock Works fork that would spit damping oil in my face on every bump, though, the old eight-track was a welcome friend.

After a restless night's sleep, I lined up for the start of the NORBA NCS event at Mammoth Mountain. I did not warm up because I did not believe I would ever see the front of the race. It was a feeling that reminded me of going to a holiday dinner with my parents at my dad's coworker's home; I knew it was going to be uncomfortable, if not painful, and nothing good would come of it, but there was no escaping it. I looked at my heart rate monitor and was surprised to see it registering under 100 beats per minute. Usually I was so nervous on the starting line that you'd think I was in full sprint mode, but this time all was calm.

When the gun went off, I pedaled easily up the side of the group and, once climbing, was surprised to find myself quickly at the front, alongside the greats of the sport. But all of that was short-lived, and by the time the course had flattened out, I was in serious trouble. I could no longer breathe. It was a feeling I had never previously experienced. My jersey felt like a hangman's noose, and I clawed at its zipper in an attempt to relieve the pressure.

Although I was being passed like a clapped-out VW Beetle on an autobahn full of BMWs, I hung on to a faint glimmer of hope. Perhaps the 25 to 30 seconds of descending would act as a reset button, enabling me to collect myself and continue racing. But at the bottom of the hill, I was still gasping for oxygen like a beached fish. When the descent ended and pedaling resumed, nothing had changed. I climbed off my bike, but my breathing was as frantic as it had been at the top of the climb. A couple of minutes passed, but there was still no improvement. In fact, it felt like things were getting worse. I slowly made my way over to a large shade tree, leaned my bike against it, and then threw myself on the ground to assume the fetal position. When the leaders came through for the second lap, I was still in the same position and my breathing only a little less frightening. By the time they came through for lap three, I was sitting up and no longer in a state of panic but by no means comfortable. It seemed that the more I hated high altitude, the harder it hated me back.

Despite my problems in the mountains, at home in Minnesota I was riding like a champ. Sure, it was only local competition, but after more than a decade of bike racing, I felt fairly well connected to my body and could at least remember what *fit* felt like. Bicknell came out to Minnesota so we could travel together to Galena, Illinois, for the Midwest's own version of the Specialized Cactus Cup. We threw our bikes into the back of my pickup truck, along with our clothing and my BB gun for post-race entertainment, and headed south.

I fully expected to see the cream of the local mountain bike race scene crop show up, but I was surprised to see that Specialized had seen fit to fly in Ned Overend, one of the sport's toughest and most prolific racers, to this regional event. My friend and former teammate Steve Tilford was also on the roster for the weekend, as was Todd Wells, a superlative athlete who would go on to become one of the cornerstones of American mountain bike and cyclocross racing.

The Cactus Cup format featured an individual time trial, a Fat Boy criterium (a downtown road criterium on slick-tire mountain bikes), and a cross-country race. As I crossed the finish for the time trial, I thought my ride was good enough for a top-five placing, but I was honestly surprised to learn I'd bested the field to take the win. Looking forward, I figured a solid ride in the Fat Boy criterium was a given, provided I could keep from crashing. And sure enough, even though I screwed up the last couple of laps on the downtown Galena circuit, I still finished on the podium.

The true test would come on the last day, when the cross-country's distance could easily reverse any time benefit I'd gained in the time trial and criterium. But whether it's the Cactus Cup or the Tour de France, leading a race is extremely motivating. When you wear the leader's jersey you become the hunted, but for however long you hold the lead, it's as if you hold a secret no one else is privy to. I was not about to give my leader's jersey up without a fight.

When the gun went off, I took care to stay near the front and watched as all the top riders did the same. Shortly into lap one, however, Jeff Hall and I put a gap on everyone else. Jeff and I had raced together so often at home that having him along was almost as good as having a teammate. I wanted to keep him with me as long as possible because I was sure the two of us together would be faster than either of us alone. But Jeff bobbled a little, and soon I was on my own.

About midway through the test, Trek rider Travis Brown caught me. Travis hadn't competed in the opening stages and wouldn't be eligible to win the overall, so I didn't need to finish near him. But it was definitely nice to have company and some-one to help keep the pace as high as possible. When Travis came by, I followed his lead. We continued on, following a script that saw me getting dropped, then catching him, then getting dropped again, then catching him again. Finally he shook me off his scent for good. He won the stage, but I won the Cactus Cup.

The season wore on, continuing its sine wave of hope and despair. I hardly even warmed up for high-altitude races anymore. Instead, since Barracuda Bicycles had run a little congratulatory blurb about my recent victory, I thought it wiser to chase a race I knew would garner some publicity: Chequamegon.

The Chequamegon 40, a mass-start, point-to-point mountain bike race that I'd already won twice, was about as important to me as the Tour of Flanders is to a Belgian bike racer. No one had taken the top step of its podium three times; I wanted to be the first. Trek, on the other hand, wanted one of its riders to win, and so it sent Marty Jemison, who had ridden his first Tour de France that year for the U.S. Postal Service Team. Also at the start were Steve Tilford, my old teammate Dave Wiens, and more than a few other strong riders.

Knowing that the Tour de France typically either makes a rider really strong or completely destroys him for the remainder of the season, I guessed Marty could most likely be beaten only in the start. Starting hard in Chequamegon had always succeeded to separate the front-runners from everyone else, so that would be my tactic once again. If I was unsuccessful in getting rid of Marty early on, I knew I'd be no match for his European road fitness.

As soon as we dropped into Rosie's Field, I lifted the tempo as high as I could and didn't look back to anyone for help. Normally I would have been on the front of the group for at least a mile before sitting up and looking back to survey the damage, but this time didn't quite work like that. We were hardly a quarter of a mile into the first section of undulating trail when the Postal Service rider passed me on the right, having apparently decided to help with the pace. As he passed, I looked to see who was on his wheel. No one was. I looked behind me to see Tilford fighting his bike as hard as possible, and though I couldn't see through Steve, I imagined Wiens to be doing the same thing. I couldn't match Marty's acceleration, and I definitely couldn't close the three-foot gap between his back wheel and my front. Perhaps sensing my struggle, Tilford put in a heroic effort that brought him and Wiens up to Jemison. I gritted my teeth, mashed the pedals, and yanked on my handlebars as hard as I could, but it was no use, and I watched helplessly as they rode away.

Somewhat dejected but not completely out, I sat up and waited for the next group to come through. There was still power in numbers at that early point in the race, and since anything was still possible up front, I jumped onto a big train of 20 or so riders and began hoping for a miracle.

The Chequamegon forest hadn't had rain for a week or more before the event, but whatever rain it had been getting before that had collected in scattered puddles that ranged from 2 feet to more than 20 feet across. The puddles were no big deal for a single-file line of riders because the correct line was always just to the side of them. Riding directly through the middle not only caused unwanted mud to collect and dry out the drive train but also risked a crash.

Heading toward our umpteenth puddle crossing of the day, I was on the wheel of my friend Dale Sedgewick, who had raced on the road as long as I. He suddenly developed a momentary lapse of reason that caused him to point his bike directly at the center of a puddle big enough to have its own lifeguard. Everything slowed down, and I could hear myself protesting, "Nooooooo." Even my voice slowed, as if in some television sitcom when one of the characters dives to catch a priceless vase that has been knocked off a table.

It was too late. Dale's bike instantly went sideways, and he crashed in front of me. I was knocked from my bike and entered the freezing water headfirst, as if sliding into second base, Pete Rose style. Before the shock of the cold water could even set in, I felt an instantly debilitating pain in my crotch that brought about incredibly clear flashbacks to my early elementary school days, when several of the little girls had learned to kick the boys between the legs. I rolled over and crawled out of the water. Former Chequamegon winner Gene Oberpriller and Dale, mostly unharmed by his crash, stayed with me to make sure I was okay. I was fine but needed a few minutes to collect myself.

Up front the mountain bike contingent of Wiens and Tilford came up short despite their solid effort to catch Tour rider Jemison. I rode the last two-thirds of the race with Geno and anyone else who wanted to ride at my pace. Interestingly, even as we dropped into the stadium barely in time to round out the top 30, I was content; I was crossing the line with my friends.

As was the case in other areas of the United States that had a strong cycling culture, the cyclocross scene in Minnesota was quickly gaining momentum. Races that would have brought out only a couple dozen riders when I moved to the Twin Cities in the fall of 1991 were now drawing upward of a hundred riders. A lighter travel schedule during the racing season left me fresher for the fall than in other years, so I decided to become more serious about cyclocross and, perhaps, go back to the national championships.

I started teaching cyclocross clinics before each race. Breaking down each step of the process was an interesting learning experience. Watching the faces of new riders who had to concentrate heavily on each individual step in the process of dismounting and remounting a bicycle—especially as they began to understand how it should feel—was at least as rewarding as the races themselves.

To supplement the weekend clinics, I started leading weeknight cyclocross training rides as well. We'd start by one of the uptown lakes and ride some road, some bike path, and some off-road. During the ride we would stop periodically and ride short laps of a "cyclocross course" at speed. If we weren't actively practicing cyclocross skills, however, we rode as slowly as possible.

I started to notice that I was losing weight and feeling really strong during the weekend races. I knew I was racing only locally and that the level of competition was not as deep as it would have been in New England, but I also knew my body and was sure that my weekend performances meant I should be absolutely flying for the national championships in Colorado.

Charles Aaron and I had been keeping the cyclocross nationals on my race calendar since the beginning of the season, and as the date drew closer I started bugging him about it more. At the start of the season the plan had been to fly me out along with a mechanic. I would take three or four bikes, two of which would be shipped ahead, with the leftover bike or bikes traveling on the plane with me. By the end of October, though, Charles began worrying about the budget, and the talk of air travel was replaced by a road trip in one of the team cars. Shortly after that, the cost of sending along a mechanic proved too much for the team's budget as well.

The course used for the 1997 Minnesota State Cyclocross Championship is one of my all-time favorites, and is reminiscent of the courses I rode in Europe. It is located in a park just a few miles from downtown Minneapolis, and its toughest obstacle is a steep staircase run-up constructed of railroad ties and other large timbers. Walking it casually, even for people over six feet tall, requires at least two or three footsteps per step, and the rise between steps is quite a bit greater than on standard steps. On previous visits to Bassett Creek Park, I would single-stride two or three of the steps and then have to double-stride a couple before feeling strong enough to take each one with just one stride again. I was fairly confident in my ability to win the race, but along with that goal I wanted to use just one stride per step, lap after lap.

When the gun went off, I managed to get a decent start and moved quickly into the top three. By the time we got to the first ascent of the stairs I had a clear view in front, but there were still a lot of guys following close behind. I shouldered my bike without losing any forward momentum and ran up the stairs, using only one stride per stair. By the third lap I was clear of the field.

In almost every race I ever entered, I would count down to the end of the race. I might count time, laps, kilometers, or miles, but I would always count. It didn't matter whether I was winning or hanging on to the roof rack of a team car on a narrow Spanish road somewhere; I always wanted the pain and suffering, or insurmountable boredom, to end, and counting was my way of reminding myself that it would. But not this time. I continued to hit my marks on each lap. I never put a foot wrong, never had a bad dismount or remount, and never slowed down. I didn't want the race to end. It wasn't international competition, but after about a thousand bike races I knew how well I had performed on the day and was really happy.

Unfortunately, the news of my ride did nothing to suddenly fill the Nautilus-Barracuda team's coffers with cash. In fact, my trip to Colorado for cyclocross had changed again. While the team vehicle was still at my disposal, I was on my own for other expenses. The hopeful young bike racer in me wanted to suck it up and make it happen, just as I had when I was starting out. Unfortunately, the jaded and sometimes bitter ex—Euro pro in me wanted none of it.

"Never use your own money to fly someone else's flag," demanded the voice inside my head.

I had raced a cyclocross bike for the last time at the Minnesota State Championship.

10

COME & GONE

SUDDENLY, QUIETLY, THE TELEPHONE CONVERSATIONS I'D BEEN having with Charles Aaron several times each week came to a halt. The chance to come back for one more season and redeem myself was fading. I had found a renewed lease on life and bike racing during the cyclocross season and was operating on the belief that there was at least a tentative agreement for me to come back to the Barracuda team—or whatever team Charles was going to be directing.

My friend Gene called me to tell me he'd heard I wasn't going to be on the team anymore. Instantly I was back in an old and all-too-familiar situation—no contract for the new season. This time, however, the situation was more dire because I had performed horrendously throughout the season, and when I hadn't shot myself in the foot, my equipment had taken care of it for me. I think I DNFed more times in 1997 than most people actually raced. With such a lackluster showing, it was going to be hard, if not impossible, to find a decent team or sponsorship package for 1998.

I started making phone calls like a fiend, begging first for the mercy of any sponsors with whom I had already worked and then reaching outside my comfort zone. Within my circle, the response was always the same: I was a week or two or three too late to get any money, and sometimes too late for equipment as well. I felt like a dog staring at a ceiling fan. I knew what I wanted to do, but I was at a loss as to how to go about it.

It didn't take long for me to realize that my career as a professional bike racer was probably finished. Although I would still hold a pro license, the likelihood of ever riding bicycles full time and traveling the world to race them was a thing of the past. But no matter how much I concentrated on that notion, there was a small part of me that absolutely would not give up, so I continued to make calls.

Ultimately a few friends within the bike industry stepped up to help me out. My friend and former teammate Dan Fox was now working for Merlin, the maker of titanium bicycle frames, and he came through with both a mountain bike and a road frame. Peter Gilbert from Cane Creek provided me with wheels, headsets, and brakes. Jeff Holt from Tioga gave seats and tires. Kurt Stockton, a former competitor on the road, gave me pedals. Sean McMahon from Troy Lee Designs sent me a helmet. Michael Herbert from Castelli, for whom I was doing a little freelance work, offered me the pick of whatever clothing I wanted. Everything else I bought.

I couldn't afford to travel anywhere in order to train for the new season; instead I spent my training time riding the rollers in the basement while staring at a bare wall or a television screen.

But with no prospect of travel to the bigger races, I had no reason to train very hard. After all, I had enjoyed some fairly easy successes for the past few years in local events. Getting myself ready for them wasn't going to be a cakewalk, but I merely divided my training time between cross-country skiing, speed skating, and evil basement roller sessions.

In early February 1998 I was still looking forward to the new season, albeit with uncertainty. I didn't know which races I would ride or how I would get to them. Since the fall I had spent a fair amount of time riding with Michael Herbert. Michael had been forming Castelli USA, a company to promote and distribute the Italian company's clothing, while winding down his now expired contract with Bianchi bicycles as U.S. sales manager. He tried to get me a sponsorship contract with Bianchi in Italy and also tried to help me find funding for my own program. Unfortunately, we were a day late and a dollar short. I had been freelancing for Michael and Castelli—doing odd jobs here and there, including making a web site—so when Michael called to say he had let his assistant go and offered me her job, I accepted, even though she had become a good friend of mine. I was to start the very next morning.

The transition to working for Michael was a bit strange. There was a time when he had wanted to hire me to race for Bianchi's American mountain bike team, but he felt there wasn't enough money in the budget. We'd also done quite a few bike rides together, so working as his assistant shifted the roles dramatically and quickly. It was as if I went to bed as a peer and woke up as a redheaded stepchild secretary.

Still, I was enjoying the distraction from the bike racer part of my life; business seemed to be a lot easier on the mind, body, and soul, so I threw myself into my new job with just about everything I had. But apart from my years as a pro cyclist, I'd never held a full-time job in my life, and adjusting to the work schedule was wreaking havoc with my training program, feeble though it was.

Quickly my fitness program devolved from a 1-to-2-hour trainer ride twice a day to a token 20-minute trainer session after work. My body, which had been starved for food and rest for the past 12 years, gratefully started storing energy in the form of fat. Although I was still skinny by any normal standard, the little bit of extra weight was pulling me further away from season-starting form.

My first race of the season was the Spring Cup at Buck Hill, a small, garbage-dump-style ski hill in Burnsville, Minnesota. Buck Hill was home to many weeknight mountain bike training races as well as other bike events, so I was intimately familiar with the possible courses. I'd also won just about every race I'd ever entered there, so I was hopeful that even with my weak fitness level I would be able to put together a decent race result.

My new employment also offered me the benefit of a nearly limitless selection of cycling apparel, which I took to the extreme at the Spring Cup. Castelli was offering an entire kit made of its silver fabric, in which microscopic flakes of actual silver were applied to white Lycra, a technology that had been developed to help dissipate heat from the bodies of Italian Olympic team cyclists during the 1996 games. Strapped into my new gear, with no sponsor logos to interrupt the expanse of fabric, I basically looked like a large, seamless silver sausage. Enhancing the effect, any portion of my skin not covered by fabric was pasty white, having attained a startling purity of tone by being drained of color through the seemingly endless Minnesota winter.

We lined up, and I assumed my rightful position at the front of the group. When the gun went off to start the race, the story changed. I had always attacked the Buck Hill course by racing flat out from the start, so I launched into this race with the same game plan. I quickly realized, though, that there was no way I was going to be able to keep up that pace this time around. I was able to ride alone for a couple laps—years of muscle memory and race-induced suffering served me well in the early going—but my lack of race fitness soon caught up with me. Still, I pushed as hard as I could, driven to attain the speed I felt I should be going versus the speed my body could handle, until finally I cracked. The mind was willing, but the body was utterly done for. All too quickly I drifted out of the top 10, and then the top 20, and finished anonymously in the middle 20s.

I was somewhat dejected, but I continued to train and think about racing. I entered what I considered to be the coolest race on the local Minnesota calendar: Millville. The race in Millville had been one of the first mountain bike races I had ever tackled, and it had never been topped as one of the most humbling experiences of my career. The race is held at Spring Creek Park, which is one of the motocross tracks that the American Motorcyclist Association uses for its outdoor national championship series. The mountain bike race follows only a short section of the motocross track before heading off into the woods for several miles of twisting, rocky, root-covered single-track. Toward the end of the lap is a long, gradual, rocky descent that is slightly reminiscent of some of the cobblestone sections in Paris-Roubaix. A quick left turn at the end of that section delivers riders into a steep, rutted, narrow chute that has many of them walking. Riding this section during my first visit to Millville scared me to death, so I viewed the fact that I had attacked the section as hard as I could on each subsequent visit as a personal achievement, one I was nearly as proud of as the world championship jerseys I'd worn.

With the memory of the disastrous season opener at Buck Hill fresh in my head, my plan was to be a bit more conservative with my energy. That was the plan, anyway. Fairly quickly I was racing with just one other rider, Jeff Hall. Jeff was one of the smoothest riders I have ever seen pedal a bike. Compared to my own big-gear-grinding style, Jeff's high cadence and fairly upright position on the bike made his race effort look easy. His bowed and unshaven legs served as a constant reminder of his hockey-playing roots and cold-weather toughness. He could start harder than just about anyone else I have ever seen, and I was often close to being dropped in the early minutes of mountain bike races that we rode together. The experience of close to a thousand bike races saw me through, however, and I was usually able to come out on top.

To this day I have no idea what transpired—whether he had a mechanical failure, a body failure, or something else, but as I had done so many times before in local and regional mountain bike races, I found myself all alone and leading the race. I put my head down and kept turning the pedals with relentless speed. At this rate it would not be a question of whether I would crack but only of *when* I would crack. If I could create enough of a gap, I might be able to stave off the inevitable charge to come from Jeff.

I was not in love with my race bike—in fact, it might be safe to say that I hated the thing. The titanium Merlin was lighter and truer-tracking than my Diamondback and Barracuda bikes had been, and in theory it was nicer than any other mountain bike I'd ridden. But I was still having trouble with it. The biggest problem was not really the bike but the suspension fork, a RockShox Sid. The Sid was, by all accounts, the lightest and most desirable cross-country fork on the market, but the thing flexed and wallowed to the point that I had no confidence in what it was going to do, and my technical cornering skills were the victim. Because of this I started attacking the little climbs harder than I should have, knowing I was not piloting the bike quickly in the bike-handling sections. On the back side of the course during the last lap, I was still in the lead, but the small power climbs were beginning to take their toll. I started to come close to blacking out each time I crested one of the little rollers. I started sneaking peeks behind to see if Jeff was in sight. Each subsequent transition from flat to climbing to downhill became harder until I finally reached the long, rocky descent that signaled that the last tough section was nearly over.

I flicked the bike left and headed down the chute. The hordes of screaming people around the course had mostly moved toward the finish line, so the final descent was a bit lonely. It was anticlimactic as well, since I was blurry-eyed and seeing stars, possessing perhaps less than half the skills I'd started the race with. As I dropped out into the deep sand at the bottom of the chute, my arms nearly collapsed, as they'd done so many times at the start of time trials during my road racing career. I pushed on slowly toward the finish and limped across the line to take the win, just seconds in front of a hard-chasing Jeff Hall. It was the last race I ever won.

I continued to work and prepare for the NORBA National at Welch Village, close to Red Wing, Minnesota. I hoped for a lucky break in the start that might help me find my way to the front of the race early on. If I could manage a decent result in this race, I might be able to find a real ride again. At that point I would have quit my job and gone back on the road in a minivan in a heartbeat.

In 1997 I had stayed at the Treasure Island Casino in Red Wing to be close to the race start, even though my house was less than an hour away. For the 1998 edition I was no longer able to afford the hotel, so Michael picked me up on race morning and we made our way to the venue. I filled the air with nervous, angry small talk and, without asking, even ate the pastries he'd brought along for himself.

Once at the track I situated my things, sorted out my bike, and pulled on my race kit. Although I tried to laugh everything off, I was more nervous for this event than any other. I was an amateur bike racer competing with pros, and that was a feeling I hadn't experienced in more than a decade.

I said my hellos, warmed up a bit, peed about a dozen times, and made my way to the staging area. Since I had absolutely no national series points, I was among the cattle herd of riders that are brought to the start area en masse instead of being called to the line by name. I paid little attention to the national anthem and final instructions from the officials. The gun went off, and I stood for a few seconds, watching the guys on the front row attack the first section of the course, before we in the back rows eventually started moving. In order to produce a solid top-10 ride, I was going to have to be able to push really hard from the start. Unfortunately, the legs weren't there. Though I was never one for the steady, solid, solitary, come-from-behind result, I continued to work my way around the course, hoping I might miraculously find some hidden power and speed.

But as the laps wore on, I knew it just wasn't going to happen. As a veteran of thousands of feed zones, I had learned to see the reflection of a good ride and good form in a soigneur's face, whether the soigneur was my own or one from another team. I knew most of them, after all, and their tells were never difficult to figure out. Now I could see the pity in each of their faces as I passed. I could tell by their lack of excitement that the leaders had come past them at more than twice my speed.

"Hey, you don't look like you're having any fun," I heard, recognizing the voice as my boss's but not immediately seeing his face.

Unlike most North American fans, the people found in most pro race feed zones don't serve up token encouragement; they don't tell you you're "looking good" when you're not. Instead, if you're completely out of contention in a race, they tend to look at you as if you were a once beautiful friend whose face was destroyed in a terrible accident, and you can feel their pain as they look at you or speak to you.

"I'm not," I told Michael after finally finding him in the small crowd of soigneurs and others who were massed in the feed zone. "This is stupid."

I climbed off my bike and mooched a cold bottle of water from one of the soigneurs. I leaned on my bike and watched as the riders who were even slower than I rolled through, followed shortly by the race leaders. I stared at bike racers and the empty trail for the next half hour, then made my way back down the hill to change.

Bike racing was no longer fun for me, so with as much fore-thought as I had entered the sport, I exited it.

EPILOGUE

ONLY CHAMPION BIKE RACERS GET TO RETIRE. THE REST OF US JUST quit. But no matter what the circumstances of a rider's departure from the sport of professional cycling, the transition to a life that doesn't revolve around racing and training is difficult. Many of us leave the sport like old men—we've given so much of ourselves to our chosen profession that when we step out the door, we're left empty and wondering what to do next.

When I quit racing, I was still craving a competitive outlet, so I raced BMX for a while. When that failed to quench my thirst, I started shooting pistols competitively, and then long-range rifles. Hitting a target squarely at 1,000 yards became an obsession. The concentration required for each match produced a level of exhaustion that made me feel like I'd just finished a bike race. It helped to fill a huge void for about five years; I was even beginning to have designs on yet another chance to represent my country in international tournaments. But as the time and travel became overwhelming, my job and relationships suffered, and I finally decided to give it up.

From guns I transitioned back to two-wheeled events in the form of off-road motorcycle racing. After a few close calls on motorcycles, I looked elsewhere and eventually started flying airplanes, with my sights set on aerobatic competition.

Ultimately I was brought back into the world of bicycles, the one place in the world where I am truly at home. After spending many years declaring war on my own body as well as the bodies of my fellow competitors, I am now content to ride purely for fun, enjoying the company and the scenery of roads and trails.

And no matter what, I still view cycling as the most beautiful and exciting sport in the world.

TEAM HISTORY

Europe

1986: Amateur (Belgium)

1987: Transvemij/Van Schilt (Holland)
Director: Jules de Wever

1988: Eurotop Keukens (Belgium)
Director: Florent van Vaerenberg

1989: ADR/HUMO (Belgium)
Director: Patrick Versluys

1990: ADR/IOC/ Tulip Computers (Belgium)
Director: José de Cauwer

1991: Tulip Computers (Belgium)
Director: José de Cauwer

USA Road

1992–1993: Scott/BiKyle (USA)
Director: Kyle Schmeer

1994: Coors Light Cycling (USA)
Director: Len Pettyjohn

USA Mountain Bike

1995–1996: Diamondback Racing (USA)
Director: Keith Ketterer

1997: Nautilus Nutritionals–Barracuda (USA)
Director: Charles Aaron

ACKNOWLEDGMENTS

Thanks to Dan Fox, John Eustice, Robin Morton, Mike Riemer, Bob Roll, and Hurl for jogging my memory.

And thanks to Ted Costantino for the kind edits and incredible patience.

ABOUT THE AUTHOR

Joe Parkin's life has not been without adventure. He has been an airplane pilot, a motorcycle racer, a sharpshooter, and of course a professional cyclist in Belgium. While racing in Europe, he represented the United States at the World Professional Road Cycling Championships and the World Cyclocross Championships. Following his road racing years in Belgium, he returned to the United States, began a successful second career as a pro mountain bike racer, and carried the stars and stripes at the World Professional Mountain Bike Championships. Parkin is the editor of *BIKE Magazine*, writes a column for Versus.com (www. versus.com/blogs/in-the-know), and maintains his own blog at 6yearsinaraincape.com.